101

DESSERTS TO

eat

BEFORE

YOU

DIE(t)

101

DESSERTS TO

eat

BEFORE

YOU

DIE(t)

Contents

INTRODUCTION

101 ways to indulge

There's no doubt that most of us don't need much of an excuse to over-indulge—especially those of us with a sweet tooth. And it's so easy to justify the excesses: if an apple a day keeps the doctor away, apple pie can only be good for you, surely? And chocolate contains anti-oxidants, so that's practically a health food too. Not to mention cream, yogurt, and other dairy products; all that calcium!

The term "sweet tooth" dates to the 1300s, but humans have probably enjoyed sweet foods for much longer than that. Early humans would have relied on fruit for much of their diet, and with fruit, sweetness equals ripeness. It's likely that humans soon learned sweet foods were both fit to eat, and tasty.

Most of us still enjoy sweet things from time to time—when we're celebrating, commiserating, congregating, or just when we want a little something sweet to round out a meal. As it seems that seeking out sweet foods is just part of being human, perhaps we should give in and do as the old saying advises: eat, drink, and be merry, for tomorrow we may diet.

SWEET, CREAMY, & Sticky DELIGHTS

Banana fritters
with butterscotch sauce

butterscotch sauce

¼ cup unsalted butter

⅓ cup dark corn syrup

⅓ cup soft brown sugar

¼ cup superfine sugar

⅔ cup whipping cream

½ teaspoon natural vanilla extract

batter

1 cup self-rising flour

1 egg, at room temperature, beaten

¾ cup soda water

1 heaping tablespoon unsalted butter, melted

oil, for deep-frying

4 firm medium bananas

confectioners' sugar, for dusting

ice cream, to serve

It's easy to see why this fabulous dessert is a childhood favorite—melting banana in a crisp, hot casing with smooth, golden butterscotch sauce. The warm banana smells wonderful too, adding to the pleasure. You can store any leftover sauce in the refrigerator for up to 2 weeks.

To make the butterscotch sauce, put the butter, corn syrup, brown sugar, and superfine sugar in a small saucepan. Stir over low heat for 2–3 minutes, or until the sugar has dissolved. Increase the heat and simmer for 3–5 minutes, taking care not to burn the sauce. Remove the pan from the heat and stir in the cream and vanilla.

To make the batter, sift the flour into a bowl and make a well in the center. Add the egg and soda water and whisk until smooth. Whisk in the melted butter.

Fill a saucepan one-third full of oil and heat to 400°F, or until a cube of bread dropped into the oil browns in 5 seconds.

Cut each banana into thirds and add to the batter in batches. Use a spoon to coat the banana in the batter.

Using a slotted spoon, carefully lower the banana into the hot oil in batches. Cook each batch for 2–3 minutes, turning until the fritters are puffed and golden brown all over. Drain the fritters on paper towels.

Serve the fritters hot, dusted with confectioners' sugar. Accompany with ice cream and the butterscotch sauce.

serves
8–10

Amaretti semifreddo

1¼ cups whipping cream

⅔ cup confectioners' sugar

4 eggs, separated

¼ cup Amaretto

½ cup blanched almonds, toasted and chopped

8 amaretti cookies, crushed

fresh berries or extra Amaretto, to serve

Whip the cream until firm peaks form, then cover and refrigerate until ready to serve.

Line a 4 x 8½ x 1½ inch bar pan with plastic wrap so that it overhangs the two long sides.

Beat the confectioners' sugar and egg yolks in a large bowl until pale and creamy. Whisk the egg whites in a separate bowl until firm peaks form.

Stir the Amaretto, almonds, and crushed cookies into the egg yolk mixture, then fold in the chilled cream and the egg whites until well combined. Carefully pour or spoon into the lined pan and cover with the overhanging plastic. Freeze for 4 hours, or until frozen but not rock hard.

Serve the semifreddo cut into slices, perhaps with your favorite fresh fruit or a drizzle of Amaretto.

NOTE Semifreddo means "partly cold," so if you want to leave it in the freezer overnight, let it soften slightly in the refrigerator for 30 minutes before serving. The semifreddo can also be poured into individual molds or dishes before freezing.

Berry trifle

1½ cups redcurrant jelly

⅔ cup fresh orange juice

2½ cups whipping cream

1 cup mascarpone cheese

¼ cup confectioners' sugar

1 teaspoon natural vanilla
extract

¼ teaspoon ground
cinnamon

9 ounces ladyfingers

1½ cups Marsala

3¼ cups fresh raspberries

1⅔ cups large strawberries,
hulled and quartered

2⅔ cups blueberries

With all those healthful berries, could this dessert really be bad for you? Well, yes. It's the cream, mascarpone, and alcohol that tip it well over the edge. But no matter how much of it you eat, you'll still likely want a trifle more.

Melt the redcurrant jelly in a small saucepan over medium heat. Remove from the heat, stir in the orange juice, and set aside until the mixture reaches room temperature.

Put the cream, mascarpone, confectioner's sugar, vanilla, and cinnamon in a bowl and whisk with electric beaters until soft peaks form.

Cut each cookie in half crossways and dip each piece in the Marsala. Arrange half of the cookie pieces over the base of a 13-cup serving bowl, or in individual glass bowls. Sprinkle a third of the combined berries over the cookies and drizzle with half the remaining Marsala and a third of the redcurrant sauce. Spoon half the cream mixture over the sauce. Repeat the layering process with the remaining dipped cookies and Marsala, a third of the berries and sauce, and the remaining cream.

Arrange the remaining berries over the cream in a mound in the center of the bowl. Reserve the final third of the redcurrant sauce, cover, and refrigerate. Cover the trifle with plastic wrap and refrigerate overnight. Before serving, pour the reserved redcurrant sauce over the berries to glaze. (Gently reheat the sauce if it is too thick.)

Cassata alla siciliana

14 ounces madeira or pound cake

4 tablespoons sweet Marsala

1½ cups ricotta cheese

½ cup superfine sugar

½ teaspoon natural vanilla extract

5½ ounces mixed candied fruit (orange, lemon, cherries, pineapple, apricot), chopped

⅓ cup chopped dark chocolate

green food coloring

7 ounces marzipan

2 tablespoons apricot jam

2½ cups confectioners' sugar

Line a 8-inch (20 cm) round cake pan with sloping sides with plastic wrap. Cut the cake into thin slices to line the pan, reserving enough pieces to cover the top at the end. Fit the slices of cake carefully into the pan, making sure there are no gaps. Sprinkle the Marsala over the cake in the pan.

Put the ricotta in a bowl and beat until smooth. Add the sugar and vanilla extract and mix well. Add the candied fruit and chocolate and mix well. Spoon into the mold, smooth the surface, and then cover with the reserved slices of cake. Cover with plastic wrap and press the top down hard. Put the cassata in the fridge for at least 2 hours or preferably overnight, then unmold onto a plate.

Knead enough green food coloring into the marzipan to tint it light green. Roll out the marzipan in a circle until it is large enough to completely cover the cassata. Melt the jam in a saucepan with a tablespoon of water and brush over the cassata. Lift the marzipan over the top and trim it to fit around the edge.

Mix the confectioners' sugar with a little hot water to make a smooth frosting that will spread easily. Add a little green food coloring if you wish. Either pipe the frosting onto the cassata in a decorative pattern, or drizzle it over the top in a lattice pattern.

serves 6

Chunky monkey sundae

chocolate fudge sauce

⅔ cup chopped dark chocolate

¾ cup sweetened condensed milk

⅓ cup whipping cream

1½ ounces unsalted butter, diced

marshmallow fluff

1 cup white marshmallows

⅓ cup whipping cream

6 scoops chocolate-chip ice cream

6 large pretzels, broken into pieces

6 scoops praline ice cream

10 chocolate-coated peanut butter cups, chopped

6 scoops peanut butter ice cream

⅓ cup honey-roasted peanuts

This dessert is practically the definition of naughtiness: so many diet-busting ingredients in one little glass. And it's so pretty to look at, too. Could you really say no?

To make the sauce, put the chocolate, condensed milk, and cream in a heatproof bowl. Fill a saucepan one-third full with water and bring to a simmer over medium heat. Sit the bowl on top of the saucepan. Stir occasionally until the chocolate has almost melted, then remove from the heat and stir until completely smooth. Beat in the butter until it is melted and the mixture is smooth. Set aside to cool for about 20 minutes, stirring regularly.

To make the marshmallow fluff, finely chop the marshmallows, put them in a saucepan with the cream, and melt over low heat until the marshmallows are completely dissolved. Allow to cool, then refrigerate.

To assemble the sundaes, put a tablespoon of chocolate fudge sauce in each of six tall sundae glasses. Top each with a scoop of chocolate-chip ice cream, some pretzel pieces, a scoop of praline ice cream, some chopped peanut butter cups, then a scoop of the peanut butter ice cream. Press down lightly.

Dollop with the marshmallow fluff. Serve drizzled with extra chocolate fudge sauce and scattered with honey-roasted peanuts.

Crêpes suzette

So French women don't get fat? Then they're just not trying hard enough. A few more of these buttery, liqueur-soaked crêpes should do the trick.

crêpes

1⅔ cups all-purpose flour

pinch of salt

1 teaspoon sugar

2 eggs, lightly beaten

1½ cups milk

1 tablespoon butter, melted

2 tablespoons finely grated
orange zest

1 tablespoon finely grated
lemon zest

butter or oil, for frying

heaping ½ cup superfine
sugar

1 cup orange juice

1 tablespoon finely grated
orange zest

2 tablespoons brandy
or Cognac

2 tablespoons Grand
Marnier

3 tablespoons unsalted
butter, diced

Sift the flour, salt, and sugar into a bowl and make a well in the center. Mix the eggs and milk together with 1 cup water and pour slowly into the well, whisking all the time to incorporate the flour until you have a smooth batter. Stir in the melted butter. Cover and refrigerate for 20 minutes, then stir the orange and lemon zest.

Heat and grease a crêpe pan or a nonstick skillet. Pour in enough batter to coat the base of the pan in a thin even layer and tip out any excess. Cook over moderate heat for about 1 minute, or until the crêpe starts to come away from the side of
the pan. Turn the crêpe and cook on the other side for 1 minute or until lightly golden. Repeat with the remaining batter. Fold the crêpes into quarters.

Melt the sugar in a large frying pan over low heat and cook to a rich caramel, tilting the pan so the caramel browns evenly. Pour in the orange juice and zest and boil for 2 minutes. Put the crêpes in the pan and spoon the sauce over them. Add the brandy and Grand Marnier and flambé by lighting the pan with your gas flame or a match (stand well back when you do this and keep a pan lid handy for emergencies). Add the butter and shake the pan until it melts. Serve immediately.

7

serves
8

Crème brûlée

2 cups cream

¾ cup plus 1 tablespoon milk

heaping ½ cup superfine
    sugar

1 vanilla bean

5 egg yolks

1 egg white

1 tablespoon orange
    flower water

½ cup raw sugar

Preheat the oven to 250°F. Put the cream, milk, and half the sugar in a saucepan with the vanilla bean. Bring just to the boil.

Meanwhile, mix together the remaining sugar, egg yolks, and the egg white. Strain the boiling milk over the egg mixture, whisking well. Stir in the orange flower water.

Ladle into eight ½-cup ramekins and place in a roasting pan. Pour enough hot water into the pan to come halfway up the sides of the ramekins. Cook for 1½ hours, or until set in the center. Cool and refrigerate until ready to serve. Just before serving, sprinkle the tops with raw sugar and caramelize under a very hot broiler or with a blowtorch. Serve immediately.

NOTE The prosaic translation of its name—"burnt cream"—really doesn't do justice to this silky, rich dessert. To get the characteristic sugar crust without melting the cream, make sure your grill (broiler) is as hot as it can be—or use a chef's blowtorch for a professional touch.

Tropical eton mess

meringues

1 egg white, at room temperature

¼ cup superfine sugar

¼ teaspoon cornstarch

heaped ¾ cup thickly sliced strawberries

½ small red papaya, seeded, peeled, and cubed

4 passionfruit

1 tablespoon superfine sugar

1 tablespoon raspberry liqueur, such as Framboise, or orange liqueur, such as Grand Marnier, optional

⅔ cup whipping cream

scant ¾ cup Greek-style yogurt

To make the meringues, preheat the oven to 250°F and line a cookie sheet with baking paper.

Whisk the egg white until stiff peaks form. Then add 1 tablespoon of the superfine sugar and whisk for 3 minutes, or until glossy. Add another tablespoon of sugar and whisk for another 3 minutes. Add the remaining sugar and the cornstrch and whisk for 2 minutes.

Put four even-sized heaped spoonfuls of the meringue mixture on the prepared cookie sheet. Bake for 30 minutes, or until the meringues are firm on the outside. Turn off the oven and leave them in the oven until the oven is cold. Roughly crumble the meringues.

Combine the strawberries, papaya, and half the passionfruit pulp in a bowl. Stir in the sugar and the liqueur, if using. Set aside for 5 minutes, or until ready to assemble.

Just before serving, whip the cream in a bowl until thick. Stir in the yogurt. Add the fruit mixture all at once and stir until roughly combined. Spoon half the cream mixture into four 1¼ cup tall sundae glasses. Top with the crumbled meringue and then the remaining cream mixture. Garnish with the remaining passionfruit pulp and serve immediately.

serves
6

1 cup self-rising flour

½ cup unsalted butter, softened

½ cup superfine sugar

1 teaspoon natural vanilla extract

2 eggs

2 tablespoons milk

½ cup treacle or dark corn syrup, plus extra, to serve

custard or whipped cream, to serve

Sticky golden sponge pudding

Lightly grease a 4-cup pudding mold. Sit the empty mold in a large saucepan on a trivet or upturned saucer, then pour enough cold water into the saucepan to come halfway up the side of the basin. Remove the basin and bring the water to the boil.

Sift the flour into a bowl. Using electric beaters, cream the butter and sugar until light and fluffy. Stir in the vanilla.

Add the eggs one at a time, beating well after each addition, and alternating with a little sifted flour.

Using a large metal spoon, gently fold in the remaining flour, then add the milk and stir to just combine. Pour the treacle or corn syrup into the base of the pudding mold and spoon the batter over the top.

Cut a sheet of baking paper and a sheet of foil large enough to fit comfortably over the top and come halfway down the sides of the mold. Lay the baking paper on top of the foil, to form a double layer. Grease the paper, then fold a pleat in the center. Invert the double sheet over the pudding, so the greased paper is facing down, then fold it down over the edge of the pudding mold. Tie a double piece of kitchen string securely around the rim of the mold, just under the lip, and run another piece of string across the top to make a handle. Cover with a tight-fitting lid.

26

TIP If you don't have a proper pudding basin you can improvize with a sturdy ceramic mixing bowl or a toughened glass (Pyrex) bowl. One with a rim is best, so you have something to tie the string under.

NOTE Sticky golden sponge pudding is best eaten on the day that it is made. However, if you really can't manage it all in one go, zap it in the microwave (in short bursts) to eat it the next day.

Carefully lower the basin into the boiling water, onto the trivet. Reduce the heat so the water is at a fast simmer. Steam for 2 hours, checking the water every 30 minutes, and topping up to the original level with boiling water as needed.

Remove the pudding from the saucepan and test with a cake tester or by pressing the top gently—it should be firm in the center and well risen. If it is not quite cooked, cover and continue steaming until done.

Turn the pudding out onto a serving dish. Serve warm with custard or whipped cream, with warmed treacle, or corn syrup passed separately.

serves
4

Fruit skewers with rum butter

1 medium peach, peeled, pitted, and cut into 8 pieces

1 medium mango, peeled, pitted, and cut into 8 pieces

8 strawberries, hulled and halved

5½ ounces papaya, cut into 8 pieces

5½ ounces pineapple, cut into 8 pieces

2 medium bananas, cut into ¾ inch pieces

¾ cup dark rum

⅓ cup dark brown sugar

1 tablespoon butter

ice cream, to serve

Put the peach, mango, strawberries, papaya, pineapple, and banana in a bowl with the rum and sugar, and stir gently until all of the fruit is coated in the marinade. Cover and refrigerate for 1 hour.

Soak eight wooden skewers in cold water for 1 hour. Drain the marinade into a small, heavy-based saucepan and thread the fruit onto the skewers. Make sure each skewer has a good mixture of fruits and that the pieces are not crowded, otherwise they won't cook evenly.

Bring the marinade to the boil over medium heat, then reduce the heat and simmer for 5 minutes, or until it is reduced and syrupy. Remove the pan from the heat and whisk in the butter until the sauce is smooth and glossy.

Preheat a flat barbecue grill plate to medium heat and cook the skewers for 5–8 minutes on each side, or until they are golden, basting them all over with the rum glaze during the last minute of cooking. Arrange the skewers on a serving plate, drizzle them with the rum glaze, and serve warm with ice cream.

Lemon delicious ice cream

lemon curd

3 egg yolks

½ cup superfine sugar

2 teaspoons finely grated lemon zest

⅓ cup lemon juice

⅓ cup unsalted butter, chopped

½ cup grated dried coconut

4 cups vanilla ice cream

To make the lemon curd, beat the egg yolks and sugar, and strain into a heatproof bowl. Add the lemon zest, juice, and butter and sit the bowl over a pan of barely simmering water, making sure the base of the bowl does not touch the water. Stir over low to medium heat for 8–10 minutes, or until the mixture thickens and coats the back of the spoon. Do not allow to boil. Cool slightly, cover with plastic wrap, and refrigerate until cold.

Meanwhile, put the coconut in a small ungreased frying pan and stir over medium heat for 3 minutes, or until lightly golden. Set aside to cool.

Remove the ice cream from the freezer and allow to soften slightly. Tip into a bowl, add the coconut and ¾ cup of the lemon curd, and stir well. Return to the freezer and whisk every half-hour or so until frozen. Soften in the fridge for 30 minutes before serving. Any leftover lemon curd can be dolloped over the ice cream.

TIP If you don't have time to make the lemon curd, use a good-quality version from a gourmet food store, a local produce market, or a school fair.

SERVING SUGGESTION

This ice cream is particularly good sandwiched between fresh waffles. Or you can spoon it into ramekins, smooth the surface, top with extra toasted coconut, and freeze until ready to serve.

makes
4 cups

2/3 cup superfine sugar

1 cup whipping cream

6 egg yolks

2½ cups milk

1 vanilla bean, split
lengthways and seeds
scraped

waffle cones, to serve
(optional)

caramel sauce, to serve

Caramel ice cream

To make the caramel, put half the sugar in a heavy-based saucepan over low to medium heat until it dissolves and starts to caramelize; tip the saucepan from side to side as the sugar cooks to help it color evenly. Remove from the heat and carefully add the cream (it will spit and splutter). Stir over low heat until the caramel melts again.

Whisk the egg yolks and remaining sugar until light and fluffy. Put the milk, vanilla bean, and scraped seeds in a saucepan and bring just to the boil, then pour into the caramel. Bring back to the boil and pour over the egg yolk mixture, whisking continuously. Remove the vanilla bean.

Pour the custard into a clean saucepan and stir constantly over low to medium heat for 8–10 minutes, or until the mixture thickens and coats the back of the spoon. Do not allow the mixture to boil. Set aside to cool slightly, then cover and refrigerate until cold.

Transfer to an ice-cream machine and freeze according to the manufacturer's instructions. Alternatively, transfer to a shallow metal tray and freeze, whisking every couple of hours, until frozen and creamy. Freeze for a further 5 hours or overnight.

About 30 minutes before serving, transfer the ice cream from the freezer to the fridge to soften. Serve scooped into waffle cones and topped with caramel sauce.

serves
4

Rice pudding

3 cups milk

1 cup heavy cream

1 vanilla bean, split
    lengthways and seeds
    scraped

scant ¼ cup superfine sugar

¼ teaspoon ground
    cinnamon

pinch grated nutmeg

1 tablespoon finely grated
    orange zest

½ cup golden raisins

2 tablespoons brandy or sweet
    Marsala

½ cup risotto or pudding rice

Put the milk, cream, vanilla bean, and seeds in a heavy-based saucepan and bring just to the boil, then remove from the heat. Add the sugar, cinnamon, nutmeg, and orange zest, and set aside.

Put the golden raisins and brandy in a small bowl and leave to soak. Add the rice to the infused milk and return to the heat. Bring to a simmer and cook, stirring occasionally, for 35 minutes, or until the rice is creamy. Stir in the golden raisins and remove the vanilla bean at the end of cooking (reserve it for another use if you like; see Tip below). Serve warm or cold.

TIP Vanilla beans are too expensive to waste. To extend the life of a vanilla bean that you've used for infusing milk or cream, rinse and dry it, then plunge it into a jar of sugar. Leave it for a few days or weeks, then use this vanilla-scented sugar in your baking, topping the jar up with more sugar as needed.

serves
4

Sticky rice with mangoes

2 cups glutinous white rice

I tablespoon white sesame seeds

I cup coconut milk

½ cup grated palm sugar (jaggery) or soft brown sugar

2–3 medium mangoes, peeled, pitted, and sliced

¼ cup coconut cream

mint sprigs, to garnish

Put the rice in a sieve and wash it under running water until the water runs clear. Put the rice in a glass or ceramic bowl, cover it with water, and leave it to soak overnight, or for a minimum of 12 hours. Drain the rice.

Line a metal or bamboo steamer with cheesecloth. Place the rice on top of the cheesecloth and cover the steamer with a tight-fitting lid. Place the steamer over a saucepan of boiling water and steam over low to medium heat for 50 minutes, or until the rice is cooked. Transfer the rice to a large bowl and fluff it up with a fork.

Toast the sesame seeds in a dry frying pan over medium heat for 3–4 minutes, shaking the pan gently, until the seeds are golden brown. Remove from the pan.

Pour the coconut milk into a small saucepan, then add the sugar and ¼ teaspoon salt. Bring slowly to the boil, stirring constantly until the sugar has dissolved. Reduce the heat and simmer for 5 minutes, or until thickened slightly. Stir often while it is simmering, and take care that it does not stick to the bottom of the pan.

Slowly pour the coconut milk over the rice. Use a fork to lift and fluff the rice. Do not stir the liquid through, otherwise the rice will become too pasty. Let the rice mixture rest for 20 minutes before carefully spooning it into the center of four warmed serving plates. Top with the mango slices. Spoon over the coconut cream and garnish with mint sprigs and the sesame seeds.

Vanilla soufflé with raspberry coulis

1 cup milk

1 teaspoon natural vanilla extract

scant ¼ cup superfine sugar, plus extra for dusting

4 eggs, separated

¼ cup all-purpose flour

2 tablespoons cornstarch

confectioners' sugar, for dusting

Raspberry sauce

3¼ cups fresh raspberries

⅔ cup confectioners' sugar

lemon juice, to taste

Preheat the oven to 375°F. Lightly grease a 6-cup soufflé dish or six 1-cup soufflé dishes and dust with superfine sugar.

To make the pastry cream, heat the milk and vanilla extract gently until just boiling. Remove from the heat and cool slightly. Beat 2 tablespoons of the superfine sugar with the egg yolks until pale and thick, then stir in the plain flour and cornstarch. Gradually stir the milk into the egg and flour mixture. Pour the custard back into the saucepan and heat gently, beating continuously until the mixture thickens and boils. Boil for 1 minute, stirring continuously. Pour into a large bowl or shallow dish and cover with plastic wrap. Set aside to cool.

Whisk the egg whites until they are firm but not dry. Combine the egg whites and remaining superfine sugar. Fold into the pastry cream mixture. Pour into the soufflé dish and run your thumb around the inside rim of the dish, about ¾ inch into the soufflé mixture, to help the soufflé rise without sticking.

Bake for 15–20 minutes, or until soufflé is risen, set, and golden. Serve at once, dusted with confectioners' sugar.

To make the sauce, put the raspberries in a blender or food processor, and blend to a smooth purée. Take care not to over-process the mixture as it can become quite frothy. Remove any seeds and fibers by pushing the mixture through a fine metal sieve. Stir in the confectioner's sugar and add lemon juice to taste.

Baked alaska

8 cups good-quality vanilla
  ice cream

9 ounces mixed candied
  fruit, finely chopped

¼ cup Grand Marnier or
  Cointreau

2 teaspoons finely grated
  orange zest

heaping ⅓ cup finely
  chopped dark chocolate

1 sponge or butter cake, cut
  into 1¼ inch slices

3 egg whites

¾ cup superfine sugar

Line an 8 cup pudding mold with damp cheesecloth.
Soften 4 cups of ice cream enough to enable the candied
fruit to be folded in with 2 tablespoons liqueur and
1 teaspoon orange zest. Spoon into the mold, smooth over
the base and up the sides, then put in the freezer until
frozen. Soften the remaining ice cream and fold in the
almonds, chocolate, remaining liqueur, and orange zest.
Spoon onto the frozen shell and level the surface.

Work quickly to evenly cover the ice cream with a 1¼ inch
thick layer of cake. Cover with foil and freeze for at least
2 hours. Preheat the oven to 425°F. Using electric
beaters, whisk the egg whites until soft peaks form.
Gradually add the sugar, beating well after each addition.
Beat for 4–5 minutes, until thick and glossy.

Unmold the ice cream onto an ovenproof dish and
remove the cheesecloth. Quickly spread the meringue
over the top to cover the ice cream completely. Bake for
5–8 minutes, or until lightly browned. Cut into wedges
and serve at once.

TIP Partly bury an upturned
half eggshell in the top of the
meringue before baking. When
ready to serve, fill eggshell
cup with warmed brandy and
carefully set alight.

17

serves
6

Orange crème caramel

4 small oranges

1 cup milk

1 cup whipping cream

1 vanilla bean, split
 lengthways, seeds scraped

3 eggs, at room temperature

2 egg yolks, at room
 temperature

½ cup superfine sugar

caramel

1½ cups superfine sugar

Preheat the oven to 315°F and half-fill
a large roasting pan with water. Carefully place the
roasting pan in the oven.

Grate the zest of two of the oranges, then peel all the
oranges, removing the rind and all the pith. Cut each
orange into six slices, discarding any seeds, and place
in a flat, heatproof dish.

To make the caramel, put the sugar and ¾ cup water in
a small saucepan over medium heat. Stir constantly for
5 minutes, or until the sugar has completely dissolved.
Brush any undissolved sugar crystals from the side of the
saucepan with a wet pastry brush. When the sugar has
dissolved, increase the heat and boil, without stirring, for
6–7 minutes, or until the mixture is golden brown.

Pour the caramel into the base of six ¾ cup ovenproof
ramekins, reserving about ½ cup of the caramel. Quickly,
but carefully, stir 1 tablespoon of water into the reserved
caramel and pour over the oranges. Cover and refrigerate
the oranges.

Put the milk, cream, vanilla bean, vanilla seeds, and
orange zest in a saucepan. Slowly bring to the boil,
then remove from the heat and set aside to infuse for
10 minutes. Beat the eggs, egg yolks, and sugar in a bowl
with electric beaters for 2–3 minutes, or until pale and

TIP You could also make this dessert in a cake pan. Use a shallow round pan about 7 inches in diameter, such as a sandwich pan. If you use a deep pan the crème caramel is more likely to splash and crack as you unmold it. Cut into wedges and serve with orange slices and a few spoonfuls of the caramel.

creamy. Strain the milk mixture over the egg mixture and beat until smooth. Pour the mixture into the ramekins containing the caramel. Put the ramekins into the roasting pan of water and bake for 45 minutes, or until a knife inserted into the center comes out clean. Cover the ramekins with foil if the surface is browning too quickly, making sure the foil doesn't touch the surface. Remove the ramekins from the roasting pan and set aside to cool, then cover and refrigerate for several hours, or overnight.

Remove the crème caramels and sliced oranges from the refrigerator 30 minutes before serving. Unmold the crème caramels onto plates and serve with the oranges.

serves
4

5 eggs, separated

heaping ¼ cup superfine
   sugar

1 cup mascarpone cheese

1 cup cold, very strong coffee

3 tablespoons brandy or sweet
   Marsala

44 small ladyfinger cookies

²/₃ cup finely grated dark
   chocolate

Tiramisu

Tiramisu translates as "pick me up." And although its eggy, sugary creaminess won't do your waistline any favors, it's sure to live up to its name by raising your spirits.

Beat the egg yolks with the sugar until the sugar has dissolved and the mixture is light and fluffy and leaves a ribbon trail when dropped from the whisk. Add the mascarpone and beat until the mixture is smooth. Whisk the egg whites in a clean, dry bowl until soft peaks form. Fold into the mascarpone mixture.

Pour the coffee into a shallow dish and add the brandy. Dip some of the ladyfingers into the coffee mixture, using enough cookies to cover the base of a 10-inch square dish. They should be fairly well soaked on both sides but not so much so that they break up. Arrange the cookies in one tightly packed layer in the base of the dish.

Spread half the mascarpone mixture over the layer of cookies. Add another layer of soaked cookies and then another layer of mascarpone, smoothing the top layer neatly. Leave to rest in the fridge for at least 2 hours or overnight. Dust with the grated chocolate to serve.

Sticky date pudding

1¼ cups chopped, pitted dates

1 teaspoon baking soda

heaping ⅓ cup unsalted butter, softened

¾ cup superfine sugar

2 eggs, lightly beaten

1 teaspoon natural vanilla extract

1½ cups self-rising flour

whipped cream and fresh raspberries, to serve

sauce

1 cup soft brown sugar

½ cup whipping cream

heaping ⅓ cup unsalted butter

Whenever you feel the need for comfort food, this gloriously gooey concoction should fit the bill. And if you're feeling particularly mopey, you might even be able to justify a double helping of sauce.

Preheat the oven to 350°F. Lightly grease an 8-inch square cake pan. Line the base with baking paper. Combine the dates with 1 cup water in a small saucepan. Bring to the boil and remove from the heat. Stir in the baking soda and set aside to cool to room temperature.

Using electric beaters, beat the butter and sugar in a small bowl until light and creamy. Add the egg gradually, beating thoroughly after each addition. Add the vanilla and beat until combined. Transfer to a large bowl.

Using a metal spoon, fold in the flour and dates with the liquid, and stir until just combined—do not overbeat. Pour into the prepared pan and bake for 50 minutes, or until a skewer comes out clean when inserted into the center of the pudding. Leave in the pan for 10 minutes before turning out.

To make the sauce, combine the sugar, cream, and butter in a small saucepan. Stir until the butter melts and the sugar dissolves. Bring to the boil, then reduce the heat and simmer for 2 minutes. Pour over slices of pudding and serve immediately, with whipped cream and raspberries (if desired).

serves
6–8

Fresh fruit pavlova

6 egg whites

2⅓ cups superfine sugar

1½ tablespoons cornstarch

1½ teaspoons vinegar

2 cups whipping cream, whipped

2 bananas, sliced

3⅓ cups strawberries, sliced

4 kiwi fruit, sliced

pulp of 4 passionfruit

Preheat the oven to 300°F. Line a large cookie sheet with baking paper. Draw a 10½ inch circle on the paper, turn the paper over, and place on the tray. Whisk the egg whites using electric beaters in a large, dry bowl until soft peaks form. Gradually add all but 2 tablespoons of the sugar, beating well after each addition. Combine the cornstarch and vinegar with the last of the sugar and beat for 1 minute before adding it to the bowl. Beat for 5–10 minutes, or until all the sugar has dissolved and the meringue is stiff and glossy. Spread onto the paper inside the circle. Shape the meringue evenly, running the flat side of a palette knife along the edge and over the top.

Bake for 40 minutes, or until pale and crisp. Reduce the heat to 235°F and bake for a further 15 minutes. Turn off the oven and cool the pavlova in the oven, keeping the door slightly ajar. When cooled, top with whipped cream, bananas, strawberries, and kiwi fruit. Drizzle with passionfruit pulp and serve.

NOTE This dessert was named in honor of the ballerina Anna Pavlova, although Australia and New Zealand can't agree over which country invented it. What's not in doubt is how delightful it is. Strawberries and passionfruit are a traditional topping, but most soft fruits can be substituted.

serves 4

Churros and chocolate

½ cup sugar

1 teaspoon ground cinnamon

2 tablespoons butter

1¼ cups all-purpose flour

½ teaspoon finely grated orange zest

¼ teaspoon superfine sugar

2 eggs

vegetable or mild olive oil, for deep-frying

hot chocolate

2 tablespoons cornstarch

4 cups milk, plus 2 tablespoons, extra

1⅓ cups chopped good-quality dark chocolate

sugar, to taste

Combine the sugar and cinnamon and spread on a plate.

Put the butter, flour, orange zest, sugar, ⅔ cup water, and a pinch of salt in a heavy-based saucepan. Stir over low heat until the butter softens and the mixture forms a dough. Cook for 2–3 minutes more, stirring, until the dough forms a ball around the spoon and leaves a coating on the base of the pan.

Transfer to a food processor and, with the motor running, add the eggs. Do not overprocess. If the dough is too soft to snip with scissors, return it to the pan and cook, stirring, over low heat until it is firmer. Spoon into a piping bag fitted with a ¼-inch star nozzle.

Heat the oil in a saucepan to 350°F, or until a cube of bread browns in 15 seconds. Pipe 2½–3¼ inch lengths of batter into the oil, a few at a time. Pipe with one hand and cut the batter off, using scissors, with the other hand. Cook for about 3 minutes, or until puffed and golden, turning once or twice. Drain on paper towels. While still hot, toss the churros in the sugar and cinnamon mixture and serve at once.

To make hot chocolate, mix cornstarch and 2 tablespoons of milk to a smooth paste. Put chocolate and remaining milk in a saucepan and whisk constantly over low heat until just warm. Stir 2 tablespoons of milk mixture into the cornstarch paste, then return all the paste to the milk. Whisking constantly, cook the mixture until it just begins to boil. Remove from the heat, add sugar to taste, and whisk for another minute. Serve with the hot churros.

makes
20

Doughnuts

2 teaspoons active dried yeast

½ teaspoon superfine sugar

3 cups all-purpose flour

½ teaspoon salt

vegetable oil, for deep-frying

superfine sugar, to serve
   (optional)

ground cinnamon, to serve
   (optional)

Dissolve the yeast in ½ cup lukewarm water and stir in the sugar. Mix the flour and salt in a mixing bowl and make a well in the center. Pour in the yeast mixture and an extra ½ cup lukewarm water. Stir sufficient flour into the liquid to form a thin batter, and leave for 15 minutes, until bubbles form. Gradually stir in the remaining flour, then mix with your hand to form a soft dough. If too stiff, add a little more water. Knead for 5 minutes in the bowl until smooth and elastic. Pour a little oil down the side of the bowl, turn the ball of dough to coat it with oil, cover with a cloth, and leave for 1 hour, until doubled in bulk.

Punch down the dough, turn out onto a work surface, and divide into 20 even-sized portions. Lightly oil your hands and two cookie sheets. Roll each piece of dough into a smooth ball and place on a tray. Using your index finger, poke a hole in the center of each ball while on the tray, then twirl it around your finger until the hole enlarges to ¾ inch in diameter. Repeat with the other balls of dough.

Fill a large saucepan one-third full of oil and heat to 375°F, or until a cube of bread dropped in the oil browns in 10 seconds. Have a long metal skewer on hand and begin with the doughnut you shaped first. Drop the doughnut into the oil, put the skewer in the center and twirl it around in a circular motion for 2–3 seconds to keep the hole open. Fry for 1½–2 minutes, turning to brown evenly. Once this process is mastered, you can drop 2–3 doughnuts at a time into the oil, briefly twirling the skewer in the center of the first one before adding the next. When cooked, lift out with the skewer onto paper towel. Toss in sugar and cinnamon if desired.

Chocolate and caramel sundae waffles

serves 4

23

caramel sauce

½ cup superfine sugar

¼ cup whipping cream

½ tablespoon butter

Eight 3¼ inch Belgian waffles

8 scoops vanilla bean ice cream

¾ cup pecans, lightly toasted

⅔ cup roughly chopped or shaved dark chocolate (70 per cent cocoa solids)

To make the caramel sauce, combine the sugar and 2 tablespoons water in a small saucepan and stir over low heat until the sugar dissolves. Increase the heat to medium, bring to the boil, and cook, without stirring, occasionally brushing down the side of the pan with a pastry brush dipped in water, until golden. Remove immediately from the heat and allow the bubbles to subside. Carefully add the cream and butter (it may spit) and stir until smooth. Set aside and keep warm.

Toast the waffles in a toaster or according to the packet directions until warmed through.

Place two waffles on each serving plate. Top with the ice cream and half the pecans and chocolate. Drizzle on the warm caramel sauce, sprinkle with the remaining pecans and chocolate, and serve immediately.

The caramel sauce will keep, stored in an airtight container or a jar in the refrigerator, for up to 1 week. Reheat, stirring frequently, in a small saucepan over low heat until warmed through.

makes
6

Frozen zabaglione with marsala sauce

²⁄₃ cup whipping cream

3 egg yolks

½ teaspoon natural vanilla extract

¾ cup Marsala

⅓ cup superfine sugar

⅓ cup whole blanched almonds, toasted and chopped

almonds, extra, to garnish (optional)

Whip the cream to form firm peaks, cover, and refrigerate.

Put the yolks, vanilla extract, ½ cup of the Marsala, and half the sugar into a nonmetallic bowl and whisk well.

Fill a saucepan one-third full with water and bring to a simmer over medium heat. Set the bowl on top of the saucepan, making sure the base of the bowl does not touch the water. Whisk continuously for 5 minutes, or until the mixture is thick and foamy. It should hold its form when drizzled from the whisk.

Remove from the heat and stand in a bowl of ice, whisking for 3 minutes, until cool. Remove from the ice and gently fold in the whipped cream and toasted almonds. Carefully pour into six ½-cup molds or ramekins, cover with plastic wrap, and freeze for 4 hours, until firm.

Combine the remaining Marsala and sugar in a small saucepan and stir over low heat until the sugar dissolves. Bring just to the boil, then reduce the heat and simmer for 4–5 minutes, or until just syrupy; do not overcook or the syrup will harden when cool. Remove from the heat and set aside until needed.

Briefly dip the molds in warm water, then loosen with a knife. Turn out onto plates and drizzle with the sauce. Garnish with almonds, if desired.

CHOCOLATE-
LOVERS'
Paradise

Chocolate éclairs

½ cup unsalted butter

1 cup all-purpose flour,
sifted

4 eggs, at room temperature,
lightly beaten

1¼ cups whipping cream,
whipped

1 cup chopped dark chocolate

Preheat the oven to 415°F. Grease two cookie sheets.
Combine the butter and 1 cup water in a saucepan. Stir
over medium heat until the butter melts. Increase the heat
and bring to the boil, then remove from the heat.

Add the flour to the saucepan and quickly beat into the
butter mixture with a wooden spoon. Return to the heat
and continue beating until the mixture leaves the side
of the pan and forms a ball. Transfer to a large bowl and
cool slightly. Beat the mixture to release any remaining
heat. Gradually add the egg, about 3 teaspoons at a time.
Beat well after each addition until all the egg has been
added and the mixture is glossy (a wooden spoon should
stand upright in it). It will be too runny if the egg is
added too quickly. If this happens, beat for several more
minutes, or until thickened.

Spoon into an icing bag fitted with a ⅝-inch plain
nozzle. Sprinkle the cookie sheets lightly with water.
Pipe 6-inch lengths onto the trays, leaving room for
expansion. Bake for 10–15 minutes, then reduce the
heat to 350°F and bake for a further 15 minutes, or until
golden and firm. Cool on a wire rack. Split each éclair
and remove any uncooked dough. Fill the éclairs with the
whipped cream.

Put the chocolate in a heatproof bowl. Half-fill a
saucepan with water, bring to the boil, then remove the
pan from the heat. Sit the bowl over the pan, making sure
the bowl doesn't touch the water. Allow to stand, stirring
occasionally, until the chocolate has melted. Spread over
the top of each éclair.

serves 8

Chocolate fudge puddings

Can too much chocolate ever be enough? With its unseemly amounts of butter, chocolate, and cream, this might be the recipe that provides the answer.

⅔ cup unsalted butter, softened

¾ cup superfine sugar

⅔ cup chocolate, melted and cooled

2 eggs, at room temperature

½ cup all-purpose flour

1 cup self-rising flour

¼ cup unsweetened cocoa powder

1 teaspoon baking soda

½ cup milk

whipped cream, to serve

sauce

¼ cup unsalted butter, chopped

¾ chopped dark or milk chocolate

½ cup whipping cream

1 teaspoon natural vanilla extract

Preheat the oven to 350°F. Lightly grease eight 1-cup ramekins with melted butter and line the bases with rounds of baking paper.

Beat the butter and sugar until light and creamy. Add the melted chocolate, beating well. Add the eggs one at a time, beating well after each addition.

Sift together the flours, cocoa, and baking soda, then fold into the chocolate mixture. Add the milk; fold through. Pour into the ramekins until they are half full.

Cover the ramekins with buttered foil and place in a roasting pan. Pour enough boiling water into the pan to come halfway up the sides of the ramekins. Bake for 35–40 minutes, or until a skewer poked into the center of a pudding comes out clean.

To make the sauce, combine the butter, chocolate, cream, and vanilla in a saucepan. Stir over low heat until the butter and chocolate have completely melted. Pour over the pudding and serve with whipped cream.

Chocolate French toast

heaping ⅓ cup chopped dark chocolate (54 percent cocoa solids)

four ⅝ inch thick slices day-old brioche

1 egg, at room temperature

1½ tablespoons cream

1½ tablespoons milk

1 tablespoon superfine sugar

½ teaspoon natural vanilla extract

¼ teaspoon ground cinnamon

1 tablespoon butter

confectioners' sugar, sifted, for dusting

Place the chocolate in a heatproof bowl over a saucepan of simmering water, ensuring the bowl doesn't touch the water. Stir until the chocolate has melted. Remove the bowl from the heat.

Spread two slices of brioche with the melted chocolate and sandwich together with the remaining slices.

Whisk the egg, cream, milk, superfine sugar, vanilla, and cinnamon with a fork in a shallow bowl.

Soak the sandwiches in the egg mixture for 30 seconds on each side. Meanwhile, melt the butter in a large nonstick frying pan over medium heat. When the butter is sizzling, remove the sandwiches from the egg mixture, allowing any excess to drip off, and place in the pan. Cook for 2 minutes on each side, or until well browned. Cut the sandwiches in half and serve immediately, dusted with the confectioners' sugar.

TIP You can use four slices of a round crusty loaf instead of the brioche, if you wish.

serves
6

Creamy chocolate mousse

heaping ¾ cup chopped
  good-quality dark chocolate

4 eggs, separated

¾ cup whipping cream,
  lightly whipped

unsweetened cocoa powder,
  to serve

Many mousse recipes will tell you that you only need small quantities of this dessert, as it's so foolishly rich—but once you've tasted it, the line between what you need and what you want may well end up fatally blurred.

Melt the chocolate in a heatproof bowl over a saucepan of gently simmering water (make sure the base of the bowl does not touch the water). Stir the chocolate occasionally until it is melted, then remove from the heat to cool slightly. Lightly beat the egg yolks and stir them into the melted chocolate, then gently fold in the cream until the mixture is velvety.

Whisk the egg whites to soft peaks. Fold one spoonful of the fluffy egg white into the mousse with a metal spoon, then gently fold in the remainder—the secret is to use a light, quick touch.

Serve the mousse in six small wine glasses or ¾ cup ramekins. Cover with plastic wrap and refrigerate for 4 hours or overnight, until set. To serve, add a dollop of whipped cream and a dusting of cocoa powder.

NOTE A tablespoon of your favorite liqueur won't go astray in this recipe. You could try brandy, rum, Frangelico, a coffee liqueur such as Kahlúa, or Cointreau or Grand Marnier. Add it to the melted chocolate, then fold in the cream.

serves 4

Chocolate affogato

1²/₃ cups chopped dark chocolate

4 cups milk

6 eggs

½ cup superfine sugar

1⅓ cups heavy cream

4 small cups of espresso or very strong coffee

4 shots Frangelico or any other liqueur that you like

Break the chocolate into individual squares and put it with the milk in a saucepan. Heat the milk over low heat; you must do this slowly or the chocolate will seize and catch on the base of the pan. As the milk heats up and the chocolate melts, stir the mixture until you have a smooth liquid. You don't need to boil the milk, as the chocolate will melt at a much lower temperature.

Whisk the eggs and sugar together with electric beaters, in a large glass or metal bowl, until the mixture is pale and frothy. Add the milk and chocolate mixture along with the cream, and mix.

Pour the mixture into a shallow plastic or metal container and put it in the freezer. To make a smooth ice cream you will now have to whisk the mixture every hour or so to break up the ice crystals as they form. When the mixture gets very stiff, leave it to set overnight.

Scoop four balls of ice cream out of the container and put them into four cups, then put these in the freezer while you make the coffee.

Serve the ice cream with the Frangelico and coffee poured over the top.

makes
36

Choc-dipped ice cream balls

1 pound 2 ounces good-quality ice cream (use vanilla or a mixture of vanilla, pistachio and chocolate)

1 cup chopped dark chocolate

1 cup chopped white chocolate

1 cup chopped milk chocolate

2 tablespoons toasted shelled walnuts, roughly chopped

2 tablespoons shelled pistachios, roughly chopped

2 tablespoons toasted shredded coconut

Line two large cookie sheets with baking paper and place in the freezer to chill. Working quickly, use a melon baller to form 36 balls of ice cream and place on the chilled cookie sheets. Place a cocktail stick in each ice cream ball. Return to the freezer for 1 hour to freeze hard.

Place the chocolate in three separate heatproof bowls. Bring a saucepan of water to the boil, then remove the pan from the heat. Sit one bowl at a time over the pan, making sure the base of the bowl does not sit in the water. Stir occasionally until the chocolate has melted. Remove the bowl from the heat and set aside to cool. The chocolate should remain liquid; if it hardens, repeat.

Put the walnuts, pistachios, and coconut in three separate small bowls. Working with 12 of the ice cream balls, dip one at a time quickly in the dark chocolate, then into the bowl with the walnuts. Return to the freezer. Repeat the process with another 12 balls, dipping them in the melted white chocolate and the pistachios. Dip the last 12 balls in the milk chocolate, then the toasted coconut. Freeze all the ice cream balls for 1 hour before serving.

Milk chocolate panna cotta with poached raisins

31

makes
6

scant 1¼ cups whipping
   cream

¾ cup milk

2 tablespoons superfine sugar

1 cup finely chopped milk
   chocolate

2 tablespoons boiling water

2 teaspoons powdered gelatin

canola oil, to grease

poached raisins

1 cup raisins

¼ cup Pedro Ximénez

Combine the cream, milk, and sugar in a small saucepan over medium heat and bring just to a simmer, stirring to dissolve the sugar. Remove from the heat, add the chocolate, and stir until it has melted.

Place the boiling water in a small heatproof dish, sprinkle on the gelatin, and whisk with a fork until the gelatin dissolves. Set aside for 1 minute, or until the liquid is clear. Add to the hot chocolate mixture and stir until combined. Strain into a jug, cover, and place in the refrigerator, stirring occasionally, for 1 hour, or until cooled to room temperature.

Very lightly brush six ½ cup dariole molds with the oil and place on a tray. Stir the cooled chocolate mixture and divide evenly among the prepared molds. Place in the refrigerator for 6 hours, or until lightly set.

Meanwhile, to make the poached raisins, combine the raisins, Pedro Ximenez, and 2 tablespoons water in a small saucepan over low heat. Simmer gently for 5 minutes, or until the liquid is reduced and syrupy, and the raisins are plump.

Slide a palette knife down the side of each mold to create an air pocket, then turn out onto serving plates. Serve accompanied with the poached raisins.

These panna cottas will keep, covered, in their molds, in the refrigerator for up to 2 days.

serves
8

Chocolate star anise cake with coffee caramel cream

1⅓ cups roughly chopped good-quality dark chocolate

½ cup unsalted butter

4 eggs

2 egg yolks

½ cup superfine sugar

⅓ cup all-purpose flour, sifted

2 teaspoons ground star anise

½ cup ground almonds

coffee caramel cream

½ cup heavy cream

¼ cup soft brown sugar

2 tablespoons brewed espresso coffee, cooled

Preheat the oven to 375°F. Grease and line a 9-inch spring-form cake pan. Put the chocolate and butter in a bowl set over a saucepan of gently simmering water, without allowing the base of the bowl to come into contact with the water. Heat gently until the mixture is melted.

Put the eggs, egg yolks, and sugar in a bowl and beat with electric beaters for 5 minutes, or until thickened. Fold in the flour, star anise, and ground almonds, then fold in the melted chocolate mixture until evenly combined (the mixture should be runny at this stage). Pour the mixture into the prepared pan and bake for 30–35 minutes, or until a skewer inserted in the middle comes out clean. Cool in the pan for 5 minutes, then remove and cool on a wire rack.

To make the coffee caramel cream, whip the cream, brown sugar, and coffee together until soft peaks form and the color is a pale caramel. Serve the cold cake cut into wedges with a spoonful of the coffee caramel cream.

Chocolate and ricotta fritters

How do you make a chocolate mixture even more decadent than it already is? Deep-fry it and dredge it in sugar and cinnamon, that's how.

serves 4–6

33

heaping I cup fresh ricotta cheese, drained overnight

I egg

I egg yolk

2 tablespoons superfine sugar

I tablespoon brandy

⅓ cup self-rising flour, sifted

½ cup finely chopped dark chocolate (54 percent cocoa solids)

4 cups vegetable oil, for deep-frying

¼ cup superfine sugar, extra

½ teaspoon ground cinnamon

Combine the ricotta, egg, egg yolk, sugar, and brandy in a medium-sized bowl and beat with a wooden spoon until well combined (the ricotta will still be a little lumpy). Mix in the flour, then stir in the chocolate. Cover and set aside for 15 minutes.

Preheat the oven to 235°F. Line a cookie sheet with paper towel and place a wire rack on top.

Heat the oil in a large heavy-based saucepan over medium heat to 350°F, or until a cube of bread dropped into the oil browns in 15 seconds. Add teaspoons of the ricotta mixture, in batches of about ten at a time, to the hot oil. Cook, turning occasionally, for 3–4 minutes, or until golden and cooked through. Use a slotted spoon to transfer the fritters from the oil to the prepared wire rack. Place in the oven to keep warm. Repeat with the remaining ricotta mixture.

When the final batch of fritters has been cooked, drain for 2 minutes on the wire rack. Combine the extra sugar and the cinnamon in a shallow bowl. Toss the fritters, in batches, in the cinnamon sugar to coat. Place on a serving plate and sprinkle with any remaining cinnamon sugar. Serve immediately.

serves
6

Chocolate sundae

chocolate fudge sauce

²/₃ cup chopped good-quality
  dark chocolate

¾ cup sweetened condensed
  milk

⅓ cup whipping cream or
  milk

3 tablespoons unsalted
  butter, diced

¼ cup flaked almonds

4 cups vanilla ice cream

6 candied cherries

6 wafers

To make the chocolate fudge sauce, put the chocolate, condensed milk, and cream in a heatproof bowl. Fill a saucepan one-third full with water and bring to a simmer over medium heat. Set the bowl on top of the saucepan, making sure the base of the bowl does not touch the water. Stir occasionally until the chocolate has almost melted, then remove from the heat and stir until completely smooth. Beat in the butter until melted and smooth. Set aside to cool for about 20 minutes, stirring regularly.

Meanwhile, dry-fry the almonds in a frying pan over high heat for 1–2 minutes until light golden, tossing regularly.

To assemble, put two scoops of ice cream into each of six sundae dishes. Pour over chocolate fudge sauce, then scatter with the toasted almonds. Top each sundae with a candied cherry and wafer. Serve immediately.

NOTE Sundaes are all about the ice cream and the chocolate sauce, so make sure you buy the best you can afford. Avoid compound chocolate and cooking chocolate, which are inferior in taste and texture. Instead, buy good-quality eating chocolate.

makes
12

Chocolate brownie and raspberry ice cream sandwich

8 cups fresh or thawed frozen raspberries

1½ cups superfine sugar

1½ teaspoons lemon juice

6 cups vanilla ice cream, slightly softened

confectioners' sugar, for dusting

chocolate brownies

⅔ cup all-purpose flour

½ cup unsweetened cocoa powder

1⅔ cups superfine sugar

⅔ cup chopped pecans or walnuts

1⅔ cups finely chopped dark chocolate

1 cup unsalted butter, melted

2 teaspoons natural vanilla extract

4 eggs, lightly beaten

Line a large square cake pan with baking paper, leaving a generous overhang on two opposite sides. Put raspberries, sugar, and lemon juice in a blender and blend to a purée. Reserve ½ cup of the purée and fold the remainder through the ice cream. Pour mixture into the prepared pan. Freeze for 2 hours, or until firm.

Preheat the oven to 350°F. Lightly grease an 8 x 12-inch cake pan and line with baking paper, leaving the paper hanging over the two long sides. To make the brownies, sift the flour and cocoa into a bowl. Add the sugar, nuts, and chocolate. Mix together and make a well in the center. Pour the butter into the well, add the vanilla extract and eggs, and mix well. Pour into the pan, smooth the surface, and bake for 45 minutes (the mixture will still be a bit soft in the middle).

Allow the brownies to cool, then chill for at least 2 hours. Lift out, using the paper as handles. Trim and cut into twelve 2 x 3½ inch rectangles. Then, using a serrated knife, cut through the center of each brownie to form two thinner brownie slices.

Remove the ice cream from the freezer. To remove it from the pan, use the overhanging paper. Cut the ice cream into 12 rectangles, the same size as the brownies. To assemble, put 12 brownie slices on a tray, top with a rectangle of ice cream, and then another brownie slice. Smooth the sides of the ice cream to neaten, if necessary. Freeze for 10 minutes until firm. Dust with confectioners' sugar and serve with the reserved raspberry sauce.

36

serves
4–6

Chocolate bread and butter pudding

¼ cup unsalted butter

6 slices fruit loaf bread

½ cup milk

2 cups whipping cream

½ cup superfine sugar

⅔ cup chopped dark chocolate

4 eggs, at room temperature, lightly beaten

½ cup chocolate chips (milk, dark or a mixture)

2 tablespoons dark corn syrup or treacle

What was once a thrifty standby using cheap ingredients and stale bread has here been jazzed up into a sweeter, creamier, more chocolatey, and altogether more calorific version.

Preheat the oven to 315°F. Grease a 4-cup baking dish with oil or melted butter.

Spread butter on the slices of bread and cut diagonally into quarters. Place in the dish in a single layer, overlapping the quarters.

Combine the milk, cream, and sugar in a saucepan and stir over low heat until the sugar dissolves. Bring to the boil and remove from the heat. Add the chocolate and stir until melted and smooth. Cool slightly, then gradually whisk in the egg.

Pour half of the custard over the bread. Stand 10 minutes, or until the bread absorbs most of the liquid. Pour over the remaining custard. Sprinkle with the chocolate bits and drizzle with corn syrup. Bake for 40–45 minutes, or until set and slightly puffed and golden. Serve warm.

serves
4–6

Cream puffs with dark chocolate sauce

¼ cup butter, chopped

¾ cup all-purpose flour

3 eggs, lightly beaten

white chocolate filling

¼ cup instant vanilla pudding mix

1 tablespoon superfine sugar

1½ cups milk

1 cup white chocolate buttons, chopped

1 tablespoon Grand Marnier

dark chocolate sauce

heaping ¾ cup chopped dark chocolate

½ cup whipping cream

Preheat the oven to 415°F. Line a cookie sheet with baking paper. Put the butter and ¾ cup water in a saucepan. Bring to the boil, then remove from the heat. Add the flour all at once. Return to the heat and stir until the mixture forms a smooth ball. Set aside to cool slightly. Transfer to a bowl and, while beating with electric beaters, gradually add the egg a little at a time, beating well after each addition, to form a thick, smooth, glossy paste.

Spoon 2 heaped teaspoons of the mixture onto the tray at 2 inch intervals. Sprinkle lightly with water and bake for 12–15 minutes, or until the dough is puffed. Turn off the oven. Pierce a small hole in the base of each cream puff with the point of a knife and return the cream puffs to the oven. Leave them to dry in the oven for 5 minutes.

To make the filling, combine the instant pudding mix and sugar in a saucepan. Gradually add the milk, stirring until smooth, then continue to stir over low heat until the mixture boils and thickens. Remove from the heat and add the white chocolate and Grand Marnier. Stir until the chocolate is melted. Cover the surface with plastic wrap and allow to cool. Stir the custard until smooth, then spoon into an icing bag fitted with a ½-inch plain nozzle. Pipe the filling into each cream puff. Serve with the warm dark chocolate sauce.

For the sauce, combine the chocolate and cream in a small saucepan. Stir over low heat until the chocolate is melted and the mixture is smooth. Serve warm.

Chocolate croissant pudding

4 croissants, torn into pieces

heaping ¾ cup chopped
good-quality dark chocolate

4 eggs

¼ cup superfine sugar

1 cup milk

1 cup cream

3 teaspoons orange liqueur

3 teaspoons finely grated
orange zest

¼ cup orange juice

2 tablespoons roughly
chopped hazelnuts

whipped cream, to serve

Preheat the oven to 350°F. Grease the base and side of an 8-inch deep-sided cake pan and line the base with baking paper. Put the croissant pieces in the pan, then scatter over two-thirds of the chocolate pieces.

Beat the eggs and sugar together until pale and creamy. Heat the milk, cream, liqueur, and remaining chocolate pieces in a saucepan until almost boiling. Stir to melt the chocolate, then remove the pan from the heat. Gradually add to the egg mixture, stirring constantly. Next, stir in the orange zest and juice. Slowly pour the mixture over the croissants, allowing the liquid to be fully absorbed before adding more.

Sprinkle with hazelnuts and bake for 50 minutes, or until a skewer comes out clean when inserted into the center. Leave to cool for 10 minutes. Turn the pudding out and invert onto a serving plate. Slice and serve warm with a dollop of cream.

NOTE Orange liqueurs go well with all manner of chocolate cakes and desserts. Brands include Grand Marnier and Cointreau. Although they're not cheap, a little goes a long way, so one bottle can last for years.

The perfect chocolate soufflé

makes
6

1¼ cups chopped good-quality dark chocolate

5 eggs, separated

¼ cup superfine sugar, plus extra for coating

2 egg whites

confectioners' sugar, for dusting

NOTE

Soufflés can be sweet or savory. A sweet soufflé has a custard or fruit purée base, to which other ingredients are added. Once a soufflé mixture is made, it must be baked immediately and then served at once.

Preheat the oven to 400°F and put a cookie sheet in the oven to preheat. Wrap a double layer of baking paper around the outside of six 1-cup ramekins to come 1¼ inches above the rim and secure with kitchen string. This encourages the soufflé to rise well. Brush the insides of the ramekins with melted butter and sprinkle with superfine sugar, shaking to coat evenly and tipping out any excess. This layer of butter and sugar helps the soufflé to grip the sides and rise as it cooks.

Put the chocolate in a large heatproof bowl. Place over a saucepan of simmering water, making sure the base of the bowl doesn't touch the water. Stir until the chocolate is melted and smooth, then remove the bowl from the saucepan. Lightly beat the egg yolks, then stir them into the sugar. Stir this mixture into the chocolate.

Whisk the egg whites using electric beaters until firm peaks form. Gently fold one-third of the whites into the chocolate mixture to loosen it. Then, using a metal spoon, fold in the remaining egg whites until just combined. Spoon the mixture into the prepared ramekins and run your thumb around the inside rim of the dish and the edge of the mixture. This helps the soufflé rise evenly. Place the ramekins on the preheated tray and bake for 12–15 minutes, or until well risen and just set. Do not open the oven door while the soufflés are baking. Cut the string and remove the paper collars. Serve immediately, lightly dusted with sifted confectioners' sugar.

40

serves
6–8

White chocolate fondue with fruit

½ cup light corn syrup

⅔ cup heavy cream

¼ cup Cointreau or other orange-flavored liqueur

1⅔ cups chopped white chocolate

marshmallows and fresh fruit such as sliced peaches, strawberries and cherries

How do you make fresh fruit bad for you? Just douse it in a sweet, alcohol-laden white chocolate sauce and serve it with marshmallows. Simple.

Combine the corn syrup and cream in a small pan or fondue pot. Bring to the boil, then remove from the heat.

Add the liqueur and white chocolate and stir until melted. Serve with marshmallows and fresh fruit, for diners to dip into the sauce.

NOTE Fondue is French for "melted," and is the name of a Swiss dish of melted cheese into which cubes of bread are dipped. This nontraditional variation is a fun dessert to serve to a crowd or as part of a buffet.

serves
8–10

Baked chocolate cheesecake

4½ ounces plain chocolate cookies

¼ cup chopped almonds

⅓ cup unsalted butter, melted

1 tablespoon soft brown sugar

filling

¾ cup chopped dark chocolate

2 cups cream cheese, at room temperature

½ cup soft brown sugar

½ cup heavy cream

2 eggs, at room temperature, beaten

1 teaspoon finely grated orange zest

whipped cream, to serve

fresh raspberries, to serve

chocolate curls, to serve

Brush an 8-inch spring-form cake pan with melted butter and line the base with baking paper. Put the cookies and almonds in a food processor and process into crumbs.

Add the melted butter and sugar and process until they are combined. Press the mixture firmly into the base of the pan and refrigerate until firm. Preheat the oven to 315°F.

To make the filling, put the chocolate in a heatproof bowl. Half-fill a saucepan with water, bring to the boil, then remove from the heat and set the bowl over the pan (don't let the bowl touch the water or the chocolate will get too hot and seize). Stir occasionally until the chocolate melts. Allow to cool.

Beat the cream cheese and sugar together until creamy. Blend in the cooled melted chocolate, cream, eggs, and orange zest and then mix until smooth.

Pour the filling over the crumb crust and smooth the surface. Bake for 1 hour 20 minutes, or until the filling is firm to the touch.

Leave the cheesecake to cool in the pan and refrigerate overnight. Top with whipped cream, raspberries, and chocolate curls. Cut into thick wedges to serve.

serves
6

Self-saucing chocolate pudding

2 teaspoons unsalted butter, melted

scant ¼ cup unsalted butter, chopped, extra

½ cup chopped good-quality dark chocolate

½ cup milk

1 cup self-rising flour

4 tablespoons unsweetened cocoa powder

¾ cup superfine sugar

1 egg, lightly beaten

½ cup firmly packed soft brown sugar

2¼ cups boiling water

confectioners' sugar, to dust

heavy cream or ice cream, to serve

Pouring boiling water over a cake batter seems all wrong – until you do it, and find that it creates a delectable sauce under a layer of rich pudding.

Preheat the oven to 350°F. Lightly grease an 8-cup ovenproof dish with melted butter.

Place the chopped butter, chocolate, and milk in a small saucepan and stir over medium heat for 3–4 minutes, or until the butter and chocolate have melted. Remove the pan from the heat and allow to cool slightly.

Sift the flour and half the cocoa, and add to the chocolate mixture with the caster sugar and the egg, stirring until just combined. Spoon into the prepared dish.

Sift the remaining cocoa evenly over the top of the pudding and sprinkle with the brown sugar. Pour the boiling water over the back of a spoon (this stops the water making holes in the cake batter) over the top of the pudding. Bake for 40 minutes, or until the pudding is firm to the touch. Leave for 2 minutes before dusting with confectioners' sugar. Serve with cream or ice cream.

43

Chocolate ganache log

cake

heaping ¾ cup unsalted
butter, softened

⅔ cup superfine sugar

6 eggs, at room temperature,
separated

1¼ cups ground almonds

1 cup chopped dark
chocolate, melted

ganache

scant ⅔ cup whipping cream

1½ cups dark chocolate,
chopped

2 teaspoons instant coffee
granules

Preheat the oven to 350°F. Grease and line a 10 x 12-inch jelly roll pan.

Beat the butter and sugar with electric beaters until light and fluffy. Add the egg yolks one at a time, beating well after each addition. Stir in the ground almonds and melted chocolate. Whisk the egg whites in a separate bowl until stiff peaks form, then gently fold into the chocolate mixture until just combined.

Spread the mixture into the prepared pan and bake for 15 minutes. Reduce the oven to 315°F and bake for another 30–35 minutes, or until a skewer comes out clean when inserted into the center of the cake. Turn the cake onto a wire rack to cool.

To make the ganache, put the cream and chocolate in a heatproof bowl over a small saucepan of barely simmering water, making sure the base of the bowl doesn't touch the water. Stir occasionally until melted and combined. Stir in the coffee until dissolved. Remove from the heat and set aside to cool for 2 hours, or until it reaches a spreading consistency.

Cut the cake lengthways into three even layers. Place a piece of cake on a serving plate and spread with a layer of ganache. Top with another layer of cake and another layer of ganache, followed by the remaining cake. Refrigerate for 30 minutes to set slightly. Cover the top and sides of the log with the remaining ganache and refrigerate for 3 hours, or preferably overnight.

Black forest cake

¾ cup butter, softened

¾ cup superfine sugar

3 eggs, at room temperature

1 teaspoon vanilla extract

1²/₃ cups self-rising flour

⅓ cup all-purpose flour

¾ cup unsweetened cocoa powder

1 tablespoon instant coffee granules

½ teaspoon baking soda

½ cup buttermilk

⅓ cup milk

1¼ cups cream, whipped

15 ounce tin pitted cherries, drained

chocolate curls, to decorate

chocolate topping

2 cups chopped dark chocolate

1½ cups unsalted butter, softened

Preheat the oven to 350°F. Grease a 9-inch round cake pan and line it with baking paper.

Cream the butter and sugar with electric beaters until light and fluffy. Add the lightly beaten egg gradually, beating thoroughly after each addition. Beat in the vanilla. Using a metal spoon, fold in the sifted flours, cocoa, coffee, and baking soda alternately with the combined buttermilk and milk. Stir until almost smooth.

Pour the mixture into the pan and smooth the surface. Bake for 40–50 minutes, or until a skewer comes out clean when inserted into the center of the cake. Leave in the pan for 20 minutes, then turn out onto a rack to cool.

To make the chocolate topping, put the chocolate in a heatproof bowl. Half-fill a saucepan with water and bring to the boil. Set the bowl over the pan but don't let the bowl touch the water. Allow to stand, stirring occasionally, until the chocolate has melted. Beat the butter until light and creamy. Add the chocolate, beating for 1 minute, or until the mixture is smooth and glossy.

Turn the cake upside down and slice into three horizontal layers. Place the first layer on a serving plate. Spread evenly with half the whipped cream, then top with half the cherries. Continue layering with the remaining cake, cream, and cherries, ending with cake on top, cut side down. Spread the chocolate topping over the top and side using a flat-bladed knife. Using an icing bag and the remaining topping, pipe swirls around the cake rim. Decorate with chocolate curls.

45

serves
16

Jaffa triple-choc brownies

Kitchen lore has it that brownies came about when a baker forgot to add the raising agent to a cake batter. Against expectations, the result was a total success— thank goodness for happy accidents!

½ cup unsalted butter, cubed

2⅓ cups roughly chopped dark chocolate

1 cup soft brown sugar

3 eggs, at room temperature

2 teaspoons finely grated orange zest

1 cup all-purpose flour

¼ cup unsweetened cocoa powder

⅔ cup milk chocolate chips

⅔ cup white chocolate chips

Preheat the oven to 350°F. Lightly grease a 9-inch square cake pan and line it with baking paper, leaving it hanging over on two opposite sides.

Place the butter and 1⅔ cups of the dark chocolate in a heatproof bowl. Half-fill a saucepan with water, bring to the boil, then remove from the heat. Sit the bowl over the saucepan, making sure the base of the bowl does not touch the water. Stir occasionally until the butter and chocolate have melted. Leave to cool.

Beat together the sugar, eggs, and orange zest until thick and fluffy. Fold in the chocolate mixture.

Sift together the flour and cocoa, then stir them into the chocolate mixture. Stir in the remaining chocolate and all the chocolate chips. Spoon into the pan, smooth the top and bake for 40 minutes, or until just cooked. Cool in the pan before lifting out, using the paper as handles. Cut into 16 squares and serve drizzled with melted milk or white chocolate.

serves
8–10

Chocolate mud cake

1 cup unsalted butter

1⅔ cups dark chocolate, broken into pieces

2 tablespoons instant coffee powder

1 cup self-rising flour

1¼ cups all-purpose flour

½ cup unsweetened cocoa powder

½ teaspoon baking soda

2½ cups sugar

4 eggs

2 tablespoons oil

½ cup buttermilk

chocolate, extra, to decorate

glaze

1⅔ cups chopped dark chocolate

½ cup whipping cream

⅔ cup superfine sugar

Preheat the oven to 315°F. Brush a deep 8½-inch round cake pan with melted butter or oil. Line the base and side with baking paper, extending it at least ¾ inch above the rim. Stir the butter, chocolate, coffee, and ¾ cup hot water in a saucepan over low heat until melted and smooth. Remove from the heat.

Sift the flours, cocoa, and baking soda into a large bowl. Stir in the sugar and make a well in the center. Add the combined eggs, oil, and buttermilk and, using a large metal spoon, slowly stir in the dry ingredients, then the melted chocolate mixture until combined. Spoon the mixture into the pan and bake for 1 hour 40 minutes, or until a skewer inserted into the center of the cake comes out clean. Cool in the pan. When completely cool, remove from the pan.

To make the glaze, stir all the ingredients in a saucepan over low heat until melted. Bring to the boil, reduce the heat, and simmer for 4–5 minutes. Remove from the heat and cool slightly. Put a wire rack on a cookie sheet and transfer the cake to the rack. Pour the glaze over the cake, making sure that the sides are evenly covered. Decorate with the extra chocolate.

makes
24 pieces

Chocolate truffle macaroon slice

3 egg whites, at room temperature

¾ cup caster (superfine) sugar

2 cups grated dried coconut

1²⁄₃ cups chopped dark chocolate

1¼ cups whipping cream

1 tablespoon unsweetened cocoa powder

TIP When whisking egg whites, ensure that the beaters and bowl are absolutely clean and dry and that there are no traces of egg yolk among the egg whites. Any traces of fat will prevent the whites from reaching their full volume.

Preheat oven to 350°F. Lightly grease an 8 x 12-inch baking pan and line it with baking paper, leaving it hanging over the two long sides.

Whisk the egg whites until soft peaks form. Slowly add the sugar, whisking well after each addition until stiff and glossy. Fold in the coconut. Spread into the pan and bake for 20 minutes, or until light brown. While still warm, press down lightly but firmly on the side with a palette knife. Cool completely.

Place the chocolate in a heatproof bowl. Bring a saucepan of water to the boil, then remove from the heat. Sit the bowl over the pan. Don't let the bowl touch the water or the chocolate will get too hot and stiffen. Stand, stirring occasionally, until the chocolate has melted. Cool slightly.

Whip the cream until thick and gently fold in the chocolate; do not overmix or it will separate. Spread evenly over the base and refrigerate for 3 hours, or until set. Lift out from the pan, dust with the cocoa, and cut into 24 pieces to serve.

serves
8–10

Devil's food cake with strawberry cream

2¼ cups self-rising flour

⅔ cup unsweetened cocoa powder

1½ cups superfine sugar

3 eggs, lightly beaten

scant ⅔ cup unsalted butter, softened

confectioners' sugar

chocolate curls

⅔ cup chopped milk chocolate

⅔ cup chopped white chocolate

ganache

1½ cups chopped dark chocolate

¼ cup plus 1 tablespoon unsalted butter

strawberry cream

1 cup whipping cream

2 tablespoons confectioners' sugar

2 cups strawberries

1 teaspoon vanilla extract

4 tablespoons strawberry jam

2 tablespoons orange liqueur

Preheat the oven to 350°F. Grease a 9½-inch round cake pan and line the base with baking paper. Sift the flour and cocoa into a large bowl. Add the sugar, eggs, butter, and 1 cup water. Using electric beaters, beat on low speed for 1 minute. Beat on high for a further 4 minutes. Pour into the pan and bake for about 55 minutes, or until cooked when tested. Leave in the pan for 20 minutes then turn out onto a wire rack.

To make chocolate curls, put the milk and white chocolate in separate heatproof bowls and melt over hot water. Spread the chocolates separately in thin layers on a flat surface. Allow to set. Using a knife at a 45-degree angle, form long, thin curls by pushing the knife through the chocolate. Refrigerate the curls until needed.

To make the ganache, put the chocolate and butter in a heatproof bowl and melt them over (not touching) hot water. Allow to stand, stirring occasionally until the chocolate has melted. Set aside to cool slightly.

Whip the cream and confectioners' sugar together until thick. Refrigerate until needed. Set aside 8 whole strawberries; hull and chop the remainder. Just before serving, fold the chopped berries and vanilla through the cream. Mix together the jam and liqueur. Cut the cake in half horizontally. Place the bottom half on a serving plate and spread evenly with jam, then strawberry cream. Top with the other cake half. Spread the ganache over the top of the cake. Arrange the milk and white chocolate curls and the strawberries over the cake. To serve, dust the cake with confectioners' sugar and cut into wedges.

makes
28

Chocolate and glacé cherry slice

1 cup all-purpose flour

⅓ cup unsweetened cocoa
    powder

⅓ cup superfine sugar

½ cup unsalted butter,
    melted

1 teaspoon natural vanilla
    extract

2 cups finely chopped glacé
    (candied) cherries

½ cup confectioners' sugar

1½ cups grated dried coconut

½ cup sweetened condensed
    milk

¼ cup unsalted butter, extra,
    melted

¼ cup melted white vegetable
    shortening

a cup chopped dark cooking
    chocolate

1 tablespoon unsalted butter,
    extra

Preheat oven to 350°F. Lightly grease a 7 x 10½-inch baking pan and line it with baking paper, leaving it hanging over the two long sides.

Sift together the flour and cocoa into a bowl, add the sugar, butter, and vanilla, and mix to form a dough. Gather together and turn onto a well-floured surface. Press together for 1 minute, then press into the base of the pan. Chill for 20 minutes. Cover with baking paper and baking beads and bake for 10–15 minutes. Remove the paper and beads and bake for a further 5 minutes. Allow to cool to room temperature.

Combine the cherries, confectioners' sugar, and coconut. Stir in the condensed milk, extra butter, and white vegetable shortening, then spread over the base. Chill for about 30 minutes.

Chop the chocolate and extra butter into small pieces and place in a heatproof bowl. Bring a saucepan of water to the boil and remove from the heat. Sit the bowl over the pan. Don't let the bowl touch the water or the chocolate will get too hot and stiffen. Stand, stirring occasionally, until melted. Pour over the chilled cherry mixture and then chill until set. Cut into 28 squares to serve.

serves
6–8

White chocolate and berry roulade

4 eggs, at room temperature, separated

½ cup superfine sugar, plus extra, for sprinkling

1 tablespoon hot water

heaped ⅓ cup white chocolate, finely grated

½ cup self-rising flour

⅔ cup sliced strawberries

heaped ¾ cup fresh raspberries

1–2 tablespoons superfine sugar, extra, to taste

¾ cup whipping cream

2 teaspoons confectioners' sugar, plus extra, for dusting

1 teaspoon natural vanilla extract

Preheat the oven to 400°F. Lightly spray or grease a 10 x 12-inch jelly roll pan with oil. Line the pan with baking paper, allowing the paper to hang over the two long sides.

Beat the egg yolks and sugar with electric beaters for 5 minutes, or until very thick and creamy. Fold in the hot water and grated white chocolate. Sift the flour over the mixture and gently fold through until just combined.

Whisk the egg whites using electric beaters until soft peaks form. Using a large metal spoon, fold the egg whites through the chocolate mixture until just combined. Pour the mixture into the pan and bake for 12–15 minutes, or until the cake is golden brown and firm to the touch.

Put a large sheet of baking paper on a flat surface and sprinkle with the extra superfine sugar. Turn the cake out onto the sugared paper. Working quickly, trim any crisp edges and roll up from the short end with the aid of the baking paper. Set aside for 5 minutes, then unroll and leave to cool.

Meanwhile, put the berries in a bowl and sweeten them with the extra 2 tablespoons superfine sugar, or to taste. Whip the cream, confectioners' sugar, and vanilla until firm peaks form. Spread the roulade with the cream and sprinkle the berries over the top. Roll up and dust with confectioners' sugar. Cut into slices to serve.

51

makes
12

Individual white chocolate-chip cakes

½ cup unsalted butter, softened

¾ cup superfine sugar

2 eggs, lightly beaten

I teaspoon natural vanilla extract

2 cups self-rising flour, sifted

½ cup buttermilk

I²/₃ cups white chocolate chips

white chocolate, shaved, to decorate

white chocolate cream cheese frosting

²/₃ cup chopped white chocolate

3 tablespoons whipping cream

¾ cup cream cheese, softened

⅓ cup confectioners' sugar

Preheat the oven to 325°F. Lightly grease a 12-hole standard muffin pan or line with paper cases.

Beat the butter and sugar in a bowl with electric beaters until light and creamy. Gradually add the egg, beating well after each addition. Add the vanilla and beat until combined. Fold in the flour alternately with the buttermilk, then fold in the chocolate chips. Fill each muffin hole three-quarters full with the mixture. Bake for 20 minutes, or until a skewer inserted into the center of each cake comes out clean. Leave in the pans for 5 minutes before turning out onto a wire rack to cool.

To make the frosting, melt the chocolate and cream in a saucepan over low heat until smooth. Cool slightly, then add to the cream cheese and confectioners' sugar and beat until smooth. Spread the icing over the cakes and top with white chocolate shavings.

PASTRIES, PIES, & Cakes

serves
6

Apple pie

Lightly grease a 9-inch pie dish. To make the filling, put the apple, sugar, zest, cloves, and 2 tablespoons water in a saucepan. Cover and cook over low heat for 8 minutes, until just tender, shaking the pan occasionally. Drain and cool completely.

To make the pastry, sift the flours into a bowl. Use your fingertips to rub in the butter until the mixture resembles fine breadcrumbs. Stir in the sugar, then make a well in the center. Add almost all the iced water and mix with a flat-bladed knife, using a cutting action, until the mixture comes together in beads. Add more water if the dough is too dry. Gather together and lift out onto a lightly floured work surface. Press into a ball and divide into two, making one portion a little bigger than the other, then wrap in plastic and refrigerate for 20 minutes.

Preheat the oven to 400°F. Roll out the larger piece of pastry between two sheets of baking paper and use to line the base and side of the pie dish. Trim any excess pastry with a small, sharp knife. Brush marmalade over the base and spoon the filling into the shell. Roll out the remaining pastry between baking paper until large enough to cover the pie. Brush water around the rim, then lay the pastry over the pie. Trim excess pastry, pinch the edges, and cut a few slits in the top to allow steam to escape.

Re-roll pastry scraps and cut into leaves to decorate the pie lid. Lightly brush the top with egg and sprinkle with sugar. Bake for 20 minutes, then reduce the oven temperature to 350°F and bake for 15–20 minutes more, or until golden.

filling

6 large granny smith apples, peeled, cored, and cut into wedges

2 tablespoons superfine sugar

1 teaspoon finely grated lemon zest

pinch ground cloves

pastry

2 cups all-purpose flour

¼ cup self-rising flour

scant ⅔ cup unsalted butter, chilled and cubed

2 tablespoons superfine sugar

about ⅓ cup iced water

2 tablespoons marmalade

1 egg, lightly beaten

1 tablespoon sugar

serves
8

Almond filo snake

53

²⁄₃ cup ground almonds

¹⁄₃ cup flaked almonds

heaping 1¹⁄₃ cups
   confectioners' sugar

1 egg, separated, white
   beaten

1 teaspoon finely grated
   lemon zest

¼ teaspoon natural
   almond extract

1 tablespoon rosewater

2 tablespoons olive oil

2 tablespoons almond oil

9 sheets filo pastry

pinch ground cinnamon

confectioners' sugar, extra,
   to dust

NOTE The snake will keep for up to 3 days but should not be stored in the refrigerator.

Preheat the oven to 350°F. Lightly grease an 8-inch round spring-form pan.

Put all the almonds in a bowl with the confectioners' sugar. Add the egg white, lemon zest, almond extract, and rosewater to the almond mixture and mix to a paste.

Divide the mixture into three and roll each portion into a sausage 18 inches long and ½ inch thick. If the paste is too sticky to roll, dust the bench with confectioners' sugar.

Mix the oils in a bowl. Remove one sheet of filo and cover the rest with a damp dish towel to prevent them from drying out. Brush the filo sheet with the oils, then cover with two more oiled sheets. Place one almond "sausage" along the length of the oiled pastry and roll up to enclose the filling. Form into a tight coil and set the coil in the center of the pan. Repeat to make more sausages and continue shaping to make a large coil of all the sausages, joined together.

Add the cinnamon to the egg yolk and brush over the snake. Bake for 30 minutes, then remove the side of the pan and turn the snake over. Bake for another 10 minutes to crisp the base. Dust with confectioners' sugar and serve warm.

Butterscotch tart

shortcrust pastry

2 cups all-purpose flour

½ cup unsalted butter,
chilled and chopped

2 tablespoons caster
(superfine) sugar

1 egg yolk

1 tablespoon iced water

butterscotch filling

1 cup soft brown sugar

⅓ cup all-purpose flour

1 cup milk

scant ¼ cup unsalted butter

1 teaspoon natural vanilla
extract

1 egg yolk

meringue

2 egg whites

2 tablespoons superfine sugar

Preheat the oven to 350°F. Grease a deep 8½-inch tart pan. Sift the flour into a large bowl. Using your fingertips, rub in the butter until the mixture resembles fine breadcrumbs. Stir in the sugar, egg yolk, and iced water. Mix to a soft dough with a flat-bladed knife, using a cutting action, then gather into a ball. Wrap in plastic wrap and refrigerate for 20 minutes.

Roll out the pastry between two sheets of baking paper until it is large enough to cover the base and side of the pan. Trim the edge and prick the pastry evenly with a fork. Refrigerate for 20 minutes. Line the pastry with baking paper and spread baking beads or uncooked rice over it. Bake for 35 minutes, then remove paper and beads.

To make the filling, place the sugar and flour in a small saucepan. Make a well in the center and gradually whisk in the milk to form a smooth paste. Add the butter and stir with a whisk over low heat for 8 minutes, or until the mixture boils and thickens. Remove from the heat, add the vanilla and egg yolk, and whisk until smooth. Spread into the pastry case and smooth the surface.

To make the meringue, whisk the egg whites until firm peaks form. Add the sugar gradually, whisking until thick and glossy and all the sugar has dissolved. Spoon over the filling and swirl into peaks with a fork or flat-bladed knife. Bake for 5–10 minutes, or until the meringue is golden. Serve warm or cold.

serves
6

Bakewell tart

1 cup all-purpose flour

⅓ cup unsalted butter,
chilled and cubed

2 teaspoons superfine sugar

2 tablespoons iced water

filling

⅓ cup unsalted butter

⅓ cup superfine sugar

2 eggs, lightly beaten

3 drops natural almond
extract

⅔ cup ground almonds

⅓ cup self-rising flour,
sifted

½ cup raspberry jam

confectioners' sugar, to dust

Preheat the oven to 350°F. Lightly grease an 8-inch round, loose-based, fluted tart pan. Sift the flour into a large bowl and rub in the butter, using your fingertips, until the mixture resembles fine breadcrumbs. Stir in the sugar. Make a well in the center, then add almost all the water and mix with a flat-bladed knife, using a cutting action, until the mixture comes together in beads, adding more water if the dough is too dry. Gently gather the dough together and roll out between two sheets of baking paper until large enough to cover the base and side of the pan. Line the pan with the pastry, trim the edges, and refrigerate for 20 minutes. Line the pastry with baking paper and pour in some baking beads or uncooked rice. Bake for 10 minutes, remove the paper and beads, then bake the pastry for another 7 minutes, or until golden. Set aside to cool.

To make the filling, beat the butter and sugar in a small bowl using electric beaters until light and creamy. Add the egg gradually, beating thoroughly after each addition. Add the almond extract and beat until combined. Transfer to a large bowl and fold in the ground almonds and flour with a metal spoon. Spread the jam over the pastry, then spoon the almond mixture on top and smooth the surface. Bake for 35 minutes, or until risen and golden. Dust with confectioners' sugar just before serving.

Chocolate caramel slice

makes
24 triangles

Chocolate and caramel seem made for each other. This no-bake slice is ultra-rich but irresistible, and will keep for several days in the fridge—if you can keep your hands off it.

2 cups crushed plain chocolate cookies

heaping $\frac{1}{3}$ cup unsalted butter, melted

2 tablespoons grated dried coconut

$\frac{1}{2}$ cup unsalted butter, extra

14 ounce can sweetened condensed milk

$\frac{1}{3}$ cup superfine sugar

3 tablespoons maple syrup

$1\frac{2}{3}$ cups chopped dark chocolate

2 teaspoons oil

Lightly grease an 8 x 12 inch shallow baking pan and line the base with baking paper, leaving the paper hanging over the two long sides.

Combine the cookie crumbs, melted butter, and coconut in a bowl, then press into the pan and smooth the surface.

Combine the butter, condensed milk, sugar, and maple syrup in a small saucepan and stir over low heat for 15 minutes, or until the sugar has dissolved and the mixture is smooth, thick, and lightly colored. Remove from the heat and cool slightly. Pour over the biscuit base and smooth the surface. Refrigerate for 30 minutes, or until firm.

Place the chocolate in a heatproof bowl set over a saucepan of simmering water, making sure that the bowl does not touch the water. Stir occasionally until the chocolate has melted. Add the oil and stir until smooth. Spread over the caramel and leave until partially set before marking into 24 triangles. Refrigerate until firm. Cut into triangles before serving.

57

serves
8–10

Carrot cake

A most appealing way to eat your vegetables!

1 cup self-rising flour

1 cup all-purpose flour

2 teaspoons ground cinnamon

1 teaspoon ground ginger

1 teaspoon grated nutmeg

1 teaspoon baking soda

1 cup oil

1 cup soft brown sugar

4 eggs

½ cup golden syrup or dark corn syrup

2½ cups shredded carrot

½ cup chopped pecans

frosting

heaping ⅔ cup cream cheese, softened

¼ cup unsalted butter, softened

1½ cups confectioners' sugar, sifted

1 teaspoon natural vanilla extract

1–2 teaspoons lemon juice

Preheat the oven to 315°F. Lightly grease a 9-inch round cake pan and line the base and side with baking paper. Sift the flours, cinnamon, ginger, half the nutmeg, and baking soda into a large bowl. Make a well in the center.

Whisk together the oil, sugar, eggs, and golden syrup until combined. Add this mixture to the well in the flour and gradually stir with a metal spoon until smooth. Stir in the carrot and nuts, then spoon into the pan and smooth the surface. Bake for 1½ hours, or until a skewer inserted into the center of the cake comes out clean. Leave the cake in the pan for at least 15 minutes before turning out onto a wire rack to cool completely.

To make the frosting, beat the cream cheese and butter using electric beaters until smooth. Gradually add the confectioner's sugar alternately with the vanilla and lemon juice, beating until light and creamy. Spread the frosting over the cake using a flat-bladed knife. Sprinkle with the remaining nutmeg.

58

makes
12

Sicilian cannoli

To make the filling, combine all the ingredients in a bowl and mix. Add 2 tablespoons water and mix well to form a dough. Cover with plastic wrap and refrigerate.

To make the dough, combine the flour, sugar, and cinnamon in a bowl, rub in the butter, and add the Marsala. Mix until the dough comes together in a loose clump, then knead on a lightly floured work surface for 4–5 minutes, or until smooth. Wrap in plastic wrap and refrigerate for at least 30 minutes.

Cut the dough in half and roll each portion on a lightly floured work surface into a thin sheet about ¼ inch thick. Cut each sheet into six 3½-inch squares. Place a metal tube (see Note) diagonally across the middle of each square. Fold the sides over the tube, moistening the overlap with water, then press together.

Heat the oil in a large, deep frying pan to 350°F, or until a cube of bread dropped into the oil browns in 15 seconds. Drop one or two tubes at a time into the hot oil. Fry gently until golden brown and crisp. Remove from the oil, gently remove the molds and drain on crumpled paper towels. When the shells are cool, fill an icing bag with the ricotta mixture and fill the shells. Dust with confectioners' sugar and serve.

filling

2 cups ricotta cheese

1 teaspoon orange flower water

½ cup diced cedro (see Note)

heaping ⅓ cup coarsely grated or chopped dark chocolate

1 tablespoon finely grated orange zest

½ cup confectioners' sugar

dough

2 cups all-purpose flour

1 tablespoon superfine sugar

1 teaspoon ground cinnamon

3 tablespoons unsalted butter

¼ cup Marsala

vegetable oil, for deep-frying

confectioners' sugar, to dust

NOTES Metal cannoli tubes are available at kitchenware shops. You can also use ¾ inch diameter wooden dowels that have been cut into 4½ inch lengths.
Cedro, also known as citron, is a citrus fruit with a very thick, knobbly skin. The skin is used to make candied peel.

serves
6–8

1¼ cups all-purpose flour

¼ cup confectioners' sugar

heaping ⅓ cup chilled unsalted butter, chopped

heaping ½ cup ground almonds

¼ cup iced water

2 x one pound nine ounce jars pitted morello cherries, drained

I egg, lightly beaten, to glaze

superfine sugar, to sprinkle

whipping cream or ice cream (optional), to serve

Cherry pie

To make the pastry, sift the flour and confectioners' sugar into a bowl. Using your fingertips, rub in the butter until the mixture resembles fine breadcrumbs. Stir in the ground almonds, then add almost all the water. Mix with a flat-bladed knife, using a cutting action, until the mixture forms a dough. Add the remaining water if the dough is too dry. Turn the dough onto a lightly floured work surface and gather together into a ball. Roll out on a sheet of baking paper into a circle about 10½ inches in diameter. Cover with plastic wrap and refrigerate for 20 minutes.

Spread the cherries into a 9-inch round pie dish.

Preheat the oven to 400°F. Cover the pie dish with the pastry and trim the overhanging edge. Roll out the remaining scraps of pastry and use a small, sharp knife to cut out decorations. Brush the pastry top all over with beaten egg and arrange the decorations on top. Brush these with beaten egg as well, and then sprinkle lightly with caster sugar. Place the pie dish on a cookie sheet (as the cherry juice may overflow a little) and cook for 35–40 minutes, or until golden brown. Serve with cream or ice cream.

serves
8

Banoffee pie

walnut pastry

1¼ cups all-purpose flour

2 tablespoons confectioners' sugar

¾ cup ground walnuts

scant ⅓ cup chilled unsalted butter, chopped

2–3 tablespoons iced water

filling

14 ounce can condensed milk

2 tablespoons unsalted butter

1 tablespoon dark corn syrup

4 bananas, sliced

1½ cups whipping cream, whipped

⅓ cup dark chocolate, melted

To make the pastry, sift the flour and confectioner's sugar into a large bowl and add the ground walnuts. Using your fingertips, rub in the butter until the mixture resembles fine breadcrumbs. Mix in most of the iced water with a flat-bladed knife, using a cutting action, until the mixture forms a firm dough. Add more water if the dough is too dry. Turn onto a lightly floured work surface and gather together into a ball. Wrap in plastic wrap and then refrigerate for 15 minutes. Roll out to fit a 9-inch tart pan. Refrigerate for 20 minutes.

Preheat the oven to 350°F. Line the pastry base with baking paper and spread baking beads or uncooked rice over the paper. Bake for 15 minutes, then remove the paper and beads and bake for 10 minutes more, until lightly golden. Set aside to cool completely.

To make the filling, put the condensed milk, butter, and golden syrup in a small saucepan. Stir over medium heat for 5 minutes, until it boils and thickens and turns a light caramel color. Cool slightly, then arrange half the bananas over the pastry and pour the caramel over the top. Smooth the surface and refrigerate for 30 minutes.

Drop spoonfuls of whipped cream over the caramel and arrange the remaining banana on top. Drizzle with melted chocolate and serve.

serves
8–10

Cherry cheese strudel

2 cups ricotta cheese

2 teaspoons finely grated lemon or orange zest

¼ cup sugar

½ cup fresh white breadcrumbs

2 tablespoons ground almonds

2 eggs

14 ounce tin pitted black cherries

2 teaspoons cornstarch

8 sheets filo pastry

¼ cup unsalted butter, melted

2 tablespoons dry white breadcrumbs

confectioners' sugar, for dusting

Preheat the oven to 350°F. Lightly grease a cookie sheet.

Combine the ricotta, zest, sugar, fresh breadcrumbs, and ground almonds in a bowl. Add the eggs and mix well. Drain the cherries, reserving half the juice. Blend the cornstarch with the reserved cherry juice in a saucepan. Stir over medium heat until the mixture boils and thickens, then set aside to cool slightly.

Layer the pastry sheets to form a large square, by placing the second sheet halfway down the first sheet. Alternate layers, brushing each sheet with melted butter and sprinkling with dry breadcrumbs as you go.

Spoon the ricotta mixture along one long edge of the pastry. Shape into a log and top with cherries and cooled syrup. Roll the pastry around the ricotta filling, folding in the edges as you roll. Finish with the pastry edge underneath. Place on the prepared tray and bake for 35–40 minutes, or until the pastry is golden. Dust with confectioners' sugar. Serve cold, cut into slices.

NOTES If you can, buy bulk ricotta from a cheese shop or supermarket deli counter. It has a better taste and firmer texture than the processed ricotta that is sold in plastic tubs.

serves
10–12

Chocolate and peanut butter pie

1½ cups crushed chocolate cookies with cream center

scant ¼ cup unsalted butter, melted

¾ cup cream cheese, at room temperature

⅔ cup confectioners' sugar, sifted

⅔ cup smooth peanut butter

I teaspoon natural vanilla extract

I cup whipping cream, whipped to firm peaks, plus ¼ cup cream, extra

I tablespoon unsalted butter, extra

heaping ⅓ cup grated dark chocolate

chopped honey-roasted peanuts, to garnish

Of all the diet-derailing, artery-clogging desserts in the world, this might be the ultimate. With cream, cookies, cream cheese, butter, chocolate, peanut butter, sugar, and more cream, it's like a blueprint for badness. Surrender and enjoy, we say.

Combine the cookie crumbs with the butter and press into the base of a 7 x 9 x 1¼ inch dish. Refrigerate for 15 minutes, or until firm.

Beat the cream cheese and confectioners' sugar with electric beaters until smooth. Add the peanut butter and vanilla and beat together. Stir in a third of the whipped cream until smooth, then gently fold in the remaining whipped cream. Spoon into the pie shell. Refrigerate for 2 hours, or until firm.

Place the extra cream and butter in a saucepan and stir over medium heat until the butter is melted and the mixture just comes to a simmer. Remove from the heat, add the grated chocolate, and stir until melted. Allow to cool a little, then drizzle the chocolate over the top of the pie to create a lattice pattern. Refrigerate for 2 hours, or until the cream cheese filling and chocolate are firm.

Remove the pie from the refrigerator, scatter over the chopped peanuts, and serve.

serves
6

Chocolate fudge pecan pie

pie pastry

1¼ cups all-purpose flour

2 tablespoons unsweetened cocoa powder

2 tablespoons soft brown sugar

heaping ⅓ cup unsalted butter, chilled and cubed

2–3 tablespoons iced water

filling

2 cups pecan nuts, roughly chopped

⅔ cup chopped dark chocolate

½ cup soft brown sugar

⅔ cup light or dark corn syrup

3 eggs, at room temperature, lightly beaten

2 teaspoons natural vanilla extract

Preheat the oven to 350°F. Grease a 7 x 9 x 1¼-inch pie dish.

To make the pastry, sift the flour, cocoa, and sugar into a bowl and rub in the butter with your fingertips until the mixture resembles fine breadcrumbs. Make a well in the center, add almost all of the iced water, and mix with a knife, using a cutting action until the mixture forms a dough. Add the remaining water if the dough is too dry.

Lift the dough onto a sheet of baking paper. Press into a disc, cover with plastic wrap and then refrigerate for 20 minutes. Roll out the dough between two sheets of baking paper to fit the dish. Line the dish with the pastry and trim the edges. Refrigerate for 20 minutes.

Cover the pastry with crumpled baking paper and fill with baking beads or uncooked rice. Bake for 15 minutes, then remove the paper and beads and bake for 15–20 minutes, or until the base is dry. Cool completely.

Spread the pecans and chocolate over the pastry base. Whisk together the sugar, corn syrup, eggs, and vanilla in a bowl. Pour into the pastry shell and bake for 45 minutes (the filling will still be a bit wobbly, but will set on cooling). Cool before cutting to serve.

serves
6–8

Custard pie

There's something comfortingly old-fashioned about custard. In this recipe it's infused with flavorings and encased in pastry—yum.

1 vanilla bean, halved lengthways

3 cups milk

²⁄₃ cup caster (superfine) sugar

heaping ½ cup semolina

1 tablespoon finely grated lemon zest

1 cinnamon stick

3 tablespoons unsalted butter, cubed

4 large eggs, lightly beaten

12 sheets filo pastry

¼ cup unsalted butter, extra, melted

syrup

¹⁄₃ cup superfine sugar

½ teaspoon ground cinnamon

1 tablespoon lemon juice

2 inch strip lemon zest

Scrape the vanilla bean seeds into a saucepan. Add the bean, milk, sugar, semolina, lemon zest, and cinnamon stick and gently bring to the boil, stirring constantly. Reduce the heat to low and simmer for 2 minutes, until the mixture thickens. Remove from the heat. Mix in the butter. Cool for 10 minutes, then remove the cinnamon stick and vanilla bean and gradually mix in the egg.

Preheat the oven to 350°F. Cover the filo with a damp dish towel. Remove a sheet, brush one side with melted butter, and place, buttered side down, in an 8 x 12 x 1¼-inch baking pan. The filo will overlap the edges. Repeat with five more sheets, buttering one side of each as you go.

Pour custard over the filo and cover with the remaining pastry, brushing with butter as you go. Brush the top with butter. Trim the pastry to the edges of the pan. Bake for 40–45 minutes, or until the custard has puffed and set and the pastry is golden brown. Leave to cool.

To make the syrup, mix all the ingredients with ¹⁄₃ cup water in a saucepan. Slowly bring to the boil, then reduce the heat to low and simmer for 10 minutes. The syrup will thicken. Remove from the heat and cool for 10 minutes. Remove the lemon zest.

If the filo has risen above the edges of the pan, flatten the top layer with your hand, then pour the syrup over the pie. This will prevent the syrup from running over the sides. Allow to cool again before serving.

serves
10–12

New york cheesecake

½ cup self-rising flour

1 cup all-purpose flour

¼ cup superfine sugar

1 teaspoon finely grated
   lemon zest

⅓ cup chilled unsalted
   butter, chopped

1 egg

1½ cups whipping cream,
   to serve

Preheat the oven to 415°F. Lightly grease a 9-inch spring-form cake pan and line the base with baking paper.

To make the pastry, combine the flours, sugar, lemon zest, and butter for about 30 seconds in a food processor, until crumbly. Add the egg and process briefly until the mixture just comes together. Turn out onto a lightly floured work surface and gather together into a ball. Refrigerate in plastic wrap for about 20 minutes, or until the mixture is firm.

Roll the dough between two sheets of baking paper until large enough to fit the base and side of the pan. Ease into the pan and trim the edges. Cover the pastry with baking paper, then baking beads or uncooked rice. Bake for 10 minutes, then remove the baking paper and beads. Flatten the pastry lightly with the back of a spoon and bake for another 5 minutes. Set aside to cool.

To make the filling, reduce the oven to 300°F. Beat the cream cheese, sugar, flour, and orange and lemon zest until smooth. Add the eggs, one at a time, beating well after each addition. Beat in the cream, pour over the pastry, and bake for 1½ hours, or until almost set. Turn off the oven and leave to cool with the door ajar. When cool, refrigerate for 6 hours or until well chilled.

TIP To make the cheesecake easier to cut, heap the zest in mounds, then cut between the mounds of zest.

filling

3 cups cream cheese, softened

1 cup superfine sugar

¼ cup all-purpose flour

2 teaspoons finely grated
orange zest

2 teaspoons finely grated
lemon zest

4 eggs

⅔ cup whipping cream

candied zest

finely shredded zest of
3 limes, 3 lemons, and
3 oranges

1 cup superfine sugar

To make the candied zest, place a little water in a saucepan with the lime, lemon, and orange zest, bring to the boil, and simmer for 1 minute. Drain the zest and repeat with fresh water. This will remove any bitterness in the zest and syrup. Put the sugar in a saucepan with ¼ cup water and stir over low heat until dissolved. Add the zest, bring to the boil, reduce the heat, and simmer for 5–6 minutes, or until the zest looks translucent. Allow to cool, then drain the zest and place on baking paper to dry (you can save the syrup to serve with the cheesecake). Whip the cream to soft peaks, spoon over the cold cheesecake, and top with candied zest.

66

Blueberry cheesecake

½ cup unsalted butter

1 cup porridge oats

1 cup finely crushed whole wheat cookies

2 tablespoons soft brown sugar

filling

scant 1⅔ cups cream cheese

scant 1/2 cup ricotta cheese

⅓ cup superfine sugar

½ cup sour cream

2 eggs

1 tablespoon finely grated orange zest

1 tablespoon all-purpose flour

topping

1⅔ cups fresh blueberries

1 cup spreadable blackberry fruit

¼ cup cherry brandy

Brush an 8-inch round, deep, spring-form cake pan with melted butter or oil and line the base with baking paper. Melt the butter in a saucepan, add the oats and biscuit crumbs and mix well. Stir in the sugar. Press half the biscuit mixture into the base of the pan and gradually press the remainder around the sides, using a glass to firm it into place, but not all the way up to the rim. Refrigerate for 10–15 minutes. Preheat the oven to 350°F.

To make the filling, beat the cream cheese, ricotta, sugar, and sour cream in a bowl using electric beaters until smooth. Add the eggs, orange zest, and flour, and beat until smooth. Put the pan on a cookie sheet to catch any drips, pour the filling into the crust, and bake for 40–45 minutes, or until the filling is just set. Remove from the oven but leave in the pan to cool.

To make the topping, scatter the blueberries on top of the cheesecake. Sieve the spreadable fruit into a small saucepan with the brandy. Stir over medium heat until smooth and then simmer for 2–3 minutes. Carefully brush over the blueberries. Refrigerate for several hours or overnight before serving.

serves
8

Classic sponge

½ cup all-purpose flour

1 cup self-rising flour

6 eggs

1 cup superfine sugar

2 tablespoons boiling water

½ cup strawberry jam

1 cup whipping cream

confectioners' sugar, to dust

Preheat the oven to 350°F. Lightly grease two 8½-inch sandwich pans or round cake pans and line the bases with baking paper. Dust the pans with a little flour, shaking off any excess.

Sift the flours together three times onto a sheet of baking paper. Whisk the eggs in a large bowl using electric beaters for 7 minutes, or until thick and pale. Gradually add the sugar to the egg, whisking thoroughly after each addition. Using a large metal spoon, quickly and gently fold in the sifted flour and boiling water.

Spread the mixture evenly into the pans and bake for 25 minutes, or until the sponges are lightly golden and shrink slightly from the sides of the pans. Leave the sponges in their pans for 5 minutes before turning out onto a wire rack to cool.

Spread jam over one of the sponges. Whip the cream in a small bowl until stiff, then spoon into an icing bag and pipe rosettes over the jam. Place the other sponge on top. Dust with confectioners' sugar to serve.

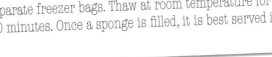

NOTES The secret to making a perfect sponge lies in the folding technique. A beating action, or using a wooden spoon, will cause loss of volume in the egg mixture and result in a flat, heavy cake.

Unfilled sponges can be frozen for up to 1 month; freeze in separate freezer bags. Thaw at room temperature for about 20 minutes. Once a sponge is filled, it is best served immediately.

makes
12

Cream buns

2 teaspoons dried yeast

2 tablespoons sugar

1⅓ cups milk, warmed

3½ cups all-purpose flour

½ teaspoon salt

¼ cup unsalted butter,
melted

½ cup strawberry jam

1¼ cups whipping cream

1 tablespoon confectioners'
sugar, plus 2 tablespoons
extra, to dust

Combine the yeast, 1 teaspoon sugar, and the milk. Leave in a warm, draft-free place for 10 minutes, or until bubbles appear on the surface. The mixture should be frothy and slightly increased in volume. If your yeast doesn't foam, discard it and start again.

Sift the flour into a bowl; stir in salt and remaining sugar. Make a well in the center, add the milk mixture and butter, and mix to a dough. Turn out onto a lightly floured work surface and knead for 10 minutes, until smooth and elastic. Place in a lightly oiled bowl, cover with plastic wrap, and leave in a warm, draft-free place for 1 hour, until well risen.

Punch down the dough and turn onto a lightly floured work surface, then knead for 2 minutes, until smooth. Divide into 12 portions. Knead one portion at a time for 30 seconds and shape into a ball.

Preheat the oven to 415°F. Lightly grease two cookie sheets, dust lightly with flour and shake off any excess. Place the balls of dough on the trays, spacing them evenly. Set aside, covered with plastic wrap, in a warm, draft-free place for 15 minutes, until the dough is well risen. Bake the buns for 20 minutes, or until well browned and cooked. Set aside for 5 minutes before transferring to a wire rack to cool completely. Using a serrated knife, make a slanted cut into the center of each bun, to a depth of 2 inches. Spread jam over the cut base of each bun. Using electric beaters, beat the cream and confectioners' sugar in a small bowl until firm peaks form. Spoon into an icing bag and pipe the cream into the buns. Dust the tops with the extra confectioners' sugar.

makes
15

Beehive cupcakes

heaping ¾ cup unsalted
    butter, softened

1 cup soft brown sugar

3 eggs

⅓ cup honey, warmed

2¼ cups self-rising flour,
    sifted

marshmallow frosting

3 egg whites

1½ cups sugar

2 teaspoons light corn syrup

pinch cream of tartar

1 teaspoon natural vanilla
    extract

yellow food coloring

15 toothpicks

15 chocolate foil-wrapped
    bumblebees with wings

Preheat the oven to 350°F. Line 15 standard muffin holes
with paper cases.

Beat the butter and sugar with electric beaters until light
and creamy. Add the eggs one at a time, beating well
after each addition. Fold in the honey and flour until
combined. Divide the mixture evenly among the cases.
Bake for 18–20 minutes, or until a skewer comes out
clean when inserted into the center of a cake. Transfer
to a wire rack to cool.

To make the marshmallow frosting, combine the egg
whites, sugar, corn syrup, cream of tartar, and scant
½ cup of water in a heatproof bowl. Set the bowl over
a saucepan of simmering water, making sure the bowl
doesn't touch the water. Beat for 5 minutes with electric
beaters, or until the mixture is light and fluffy. Remove
from the heat. Add the vanilla and beat with electric
beaters for 4–5 minutes, or until stiff peaks form. Add
the coloring, drop by drop, and beat until just combined.

Spoon the frosting into an icing bag fitted with a ½-inch
round nozzle, and pipe the icing in circles around the
cake to resemble a beehive. Push the pointy end of a
toothpick into each bee and insert into the cakes.

makes
24

Fruit mince pies

fruit mince

⅓ cup raisins, chopped

⅓ cup soft brown sugar

¼ cup golden raisins

¼ cup mixed candied citrus peel

1 tablespoon currants

1 tablespoon chopped almonds

1 small apple, grated

1 teaspoon lemon juice

½ teaspoon grated orange zest

½ teaspoon finely grated lemon zest

½ teaspoon pumpkin pie spice

pinch freshly grated nutmeg

2 tablespoons butter, melted

1 tablespoon brandy

pastry

2 cups all-purpose flour

scant ⅔ cup butter, chilled and cubed

⅔ cup confectioners' sugar, plus extra, to dust

To make the fruit mince, combine all the fruit mince ingredients in a bowl. Spoon into a sterilized jar and seal. You can use the fruit mince straight away, but the flavors develop if the mixture is kept for a while. Keep it in a cool, dark place for up to 3 months. (Alternatively, use ready-made fruit mince if you're short of time.)

Preheat the oven to 350°F . Lightly grease two 12-hole shallow patty pans or mini muffin pans.

To make the pastry, sift the flour into a bowl. Using your fingertips, rub in the butter until the mixture resembles fine breadcrumbs. Stir in the confectioners' sugar and make a well in the center. Add about 2 tablespoons iced water and mix with a flat-bladed knife, using a cutting action, until the mixture comes together in beads. Add up to 1 tablespoon extra iced water if the dough is too dry. Turn out onto a lightly floured work surface and gather into a ball. Roll out two-thirds of the pastry and cut out 24 rounds, slightly larger than the holes in the patty pans, with a round fluted cutter. Fit the rounds into the pans.

Divide the fruit mince among the pastry cases. Roll out the remaining pastry, a little thinner than before, and cut 12 rounds with the same cutter. Using a smaller fluted cutter, cut 12 more rounds. Place the large circles on top of half the pies and press the edges to seal. Place the smaller circles on the remainder. Bake for 25 minutes, or until golden. Leave in the pans for 5 minutes, then remove and cool on wire racks. Dust with confectioners' sugar.

71

Fruit tart

shortcrust pastry

1¼ cups all-purpose flour

2 tablespoons superfine sugar

⅓ cup unsalted butter, chilled and chopped

1 egg yolk

1 tablespoon iced water

filling

1 cup milk

3 egg yolks

¼ cup superfine sugar

2 tablespoons all-purpose flour

1 teaspoon natural vanilla extract

strawberries, kiwi fruit, and blueberries, to decorate

apricot jam, to glaze

To make the pastry, sift the flour into a bowl and stir in the sugar. Using your fingertips, rub in the butter until the mixture resembles fine breadcrumbs. Make a well in the center and add the egg yolk and iced water. Mix to a dough with a flat-bladed knife, using a cutting action. Turn out onto a lightly floured work surface and gather together into a ball. Press together gently until smooth, and then roll out to fit a 13½ x 4-inch loose-based fluted tart pan. Line the pan with the pastry and trim any excess. Wrap in plastic wrap and refrigerate for 20 minutes. Preheat the oven to 375°F.

Cover the pastry with baking paper, then with a layer of baking beads or uncooked rice. Bake for 15 minutes, remove the paper and beads, and bake for another 20 minutes, or until cooked and golden brown around the edge. Set aside to cool completely.

To make the filling, put the milk in a small saucepan and bring to the boil. Set aside while quickly whisking the egg yolks and sugar together in a bowl until light and creamy. Whisk in the flour. Pour the hot milk slowly onto the egg mixture, whisking constantly. Wash out the pan, return the milk mixture to the pan, and bring to the boil over medium heat, stirring with a wire whisk. Boil for 2 minutes, stirring occasionally. Transfer to a bowl, stir in the vanilla, and leave to cool, stirring frequently to

NOTE If you don't have a rectangular pan, this tart may be made in a 9-inch round tart pan. You can use different fruits to top the tart, according to your own taste and the season.

prevent a skin from forming. When cool, cover with plastic wrap and refrigerate until cold.

Cut the strawberries in half and peel and slice the kiwi fruit. Spoon the cold custard into the pastry shell, then arrange the fruit over the custard, pressing it in slightly. Heat the jam in the microwave or in a small saucepan until liquid, then sieve it to remove any lumps. Using a pastry brush, glaze the fruit with the jam. Serve the tart on the same day, at room temperature. If it is to be left for a while on a hot day, refrigerate it.

Honey cream roll

72

serves
8–10

There is something charmingly retro about a sponge roll such as this, and it makes a pretty addition to a morning tea or ladies' lunch.

¾ cup self-rising flour

2 teaspoons pumpkin pie spice

3 eggs

⅔ cup soft brown sugar

¼ cup grated dried coconut

honey cream

½ cup unsalted butter, softened

⅓ cup confectioners' sugar

2 tablespoons honey

Preheat the oven to 375°F. Lightly grease a 10 x 12 x ¾-inch jelly roll pan and line the base with baking paper, extending it over the two long sides. Sift the flour and mixed spice three times onto a sheet of baking paper. Beat the eggs in a large bowl using electric beaters for 5 minutes, or until thick, frothy, and pale. Add the sugar gradually, beating constantly until the sugar has dissolved and the mixture is pale and glossy. Using a metal spoon, fold in the flour quickly and lightly. Spread into the pan and smooth the surface. Bake for 10–12 minutes, or until the cake is lightly golden and springy to touch.

Meanwhile, place a clean dish towel on a work surface, cover with baking paper, and sprinkle the paper with coconut. Turn the cooked cake out onto the coconut. Using the dish towel as a guide, carefully roll up the cake, along with the paper, from the short side. Leave to cool.

To make the honey cream, beat all the ingredients in a bowl using electric beaters until light and creamy and the sugar has dissolved. Unroll the cake and discard the paper. Spread with honey cream and reroll. Trim the ends with a serrated knife.

Zuccotto

10½ ounce madeira or pound cake

3 tablespoons maraschino liqueur

3 tablespoons brandy

2 cups heavy cream

¾ cup confectioners' sugar

1 cup roughly chopped dark chocolate

⅓ cup chopped blanched almonds

¼ cup chopped skinned hazelnuts

1 ounce chopped mixed candied citrus peel

unsweetened cocoa powder, to dust

confectioners' sugar, to dust

Cut the cake into ½-inch slices and then cut each slice into two triangles. Combine the maraschino and brandy and sprinkle them over the cake.

Line a round 6-cup bowl with a layer of plastic wrap and then with the cake slices. Arrange the slices with the narrow point of each triangle pointing into the bottom of the bowl to form a star pattern, fitting each piece snugly against the others so you don't have any gaps. Cut smaller triangles to fit the gaps along the top and keep the rest of the cake for the top.

Whip the cream until soft peaks form and then whisk in the confectioners' sugar until you have a stiff mixture. Add about a third of the chocolate and all the almonds, hazelnuts, and candied citrus peel. Mix together thoroughly, then fill the cake-lined bowl with half the mixture, making a hollow in the middle and drawing the mixture up the sides. Refrigerate while melting the chocolate.

Melt the rest of the chocolate in a heatproof bowl over a saucepan of simmering water, or in a microwave, and fold it into the remaining cream and nut mixture. Spoon this into the bowl and then cover the top with a layer of cake triangles, leaving no gaps. Cover the bowl with plastic wrap and refrigerate overnight.

To serve, unmold the zuccotto and use a triangular piece of cardboard as a template to dust the top with alternating segments of cocoa and confectioners' sugar.

74

Lemon meringue pie

1½ cups all-purpose flour

2 tablespoons confectioners' sugar

½ cup unsalted butter, chilled and chopped

¼ cup iced water

filling and topping

¼ cup cornstarch, plus ½ teaspoon extra

¼ cup all-purpose flour

1 cup superfine sugar

¾ cup lemon juice

3 teaspoons finely grated lemon zest

3 tablespoons unsalted butter, chopped

6 eggs, separated

1½ cups superfine sugar, extra

Sift the flour and confectioners' sugar into a large bowl. Using your fingertips, rub in the butter until the mixture resembles fine breadcrumbs. Add almost all the water and mix with a flat-bladed knife, using a cutting action, until the mixture forms a firm dough. Add more liquid if the dough is too dry. Turn onto a lightly floured surface and gather into a ball. Roll between two sheets of baking paper until large enough to fit a 9-inch pie dish. Line the dish with the pastry, trim the edge, and refrigerate for 20 minutes. Preheat the oven to 350°F.

Line the pastry with a sheet of baking paper and spread a layer of baking beads or uncooked rice evenly over the paper. Bake for 10 minutes, then remove the paper and beads. Bake for a further 10 minutes, or until the pastry is lightly golden. Leave to cool.

To make the filling, put the flours and sugar in a saucepan. Whisk in the lemon juice, zest, and 1½ cups water. Whisk continuously over medium heat until the mixture boils and thickens. Reduce the heat and cook for 1 minute, then whisk in the butter and egg yolks, one yolk at a time. Transfer to a bowl, cover the surface with plastic wrap, and allow to cool completely.

To make the topping, preheat the oven to 425°F. Whisk the egg whites in a small dry bowl using electric beaters, until soft peaks form. Add the extra sugar gradually, and whisk constantly until the meringue is thick and glossy. Whisk in the extra cornstarch. Pour the cold filling into the cold pastry shell. Spread with meringue to cover, forming peaks. Bake for 5–10 minutes, or until lightly browned. Serve hot or cold.

serves
6–8

shortcrust pastry

1½ cups all-purpose flour

½ cup unsalted butter,
chilled and chopped

2–3 tablespoons iced water

filling

2 cups pecan nuts

3 eggs, lightly beaten

scant ¼ cup unsalted butter,
melted and cooled

¾ cup soft brown sugar

⅔ cup light corn syrup

1 teaspoon natural vanilla
extract

pinch of salt

Pecan pie

Preheat the oven to 350°F. To make the pastry, sift the flour into a large bowl. Using your fingertips, rub in the butter until the mixture resembles fine breadcrumbs. Add almost all the water and mix with a flat-bladed knife, using a cutting action, until the mixture comes together in beads. Add more water if the dough is too dry. Turn out onto a lightly floured work surface and gather together into a ball.

Roll out the pastry to a 14-inch round. Line a 9-inch tart pan with the pastry, trim the edges, and refrigerate for 20 minutes. Pile the pastry trimmings together, roll out on baking paper to a rectangle about $\frac{1}{16}$ inch thick, then refrigerate.

Cover the pastry in the tart pan with a sheet of baking paper and spread with a layer of baking beads or uncooked rice. Bake for 15 minutes, then remove the paper and beads, and bake for another 15 minutes, or until lightly golden. Cool completely.

To make the filling, spread the pecans over the pastry. Whisk the eggs, butter, sugar, corn syrup, vanilla, and salt until combined, then pour over the nuts.

Using a fluted pastry wheel or small sharp knife, cut narrow strips from half of the pastry trimmings. Cut out small stars with a cookie cutter from the remaining trimmings. Arrange decoratively over the filling. Bake the pie for 45 minutes, or until firm. Allow to cool completely and serve at room temperature.

76

serves
8

Pumpkin pie

Lightly grease a 9-inch round pie dish. Steam or boil the squash for 10 minutes, until just tender. Drain thoroughly, then mash and set aside to cool.

To make the pastry, sift the flour into a large bowl. Using your fingertips, rub in the butter until the mixture resembles fine breadcrumbs. Stir in the caster sugar. Make a well in the center, add almost all the water, and mix with a flat-bladed knife, using a cutting action, until the mixture comes together in beads. Add a little more iced water if the dough is too dry. Gather the dough together and roll it out between two sheets of baking paper until it is large enough to cover the base and side of the pie dish. Line the dish with pastry, trim away the excess and crimp the edges. To make decorations, roll out extra pastry to 1/16 inch thick. Cut out leaf shapes of different sizes and score vein markings onto the leaves. Refrigerate the pastry-lined dish and the leaf shapes for about 20 minutes.

Preheat the oven to 350°F. Cover the pastry with a sheet of baking paper. Spread baking beads or uncooked rice over the paper. Bake for 10 minutes, then remove the paper and beads and bake for a further 10 minutes, until lightly golden. Meanwhile, place the leaves on a cookie sheet lined with baking paper, brush with the combined egg yolk and milk, and bake for 10–15 minutes, or until lightly golden. Set aside to cool.

To make the filling, whisk the eggs and brown sugar in a large bowl. Add the pumpkin, cream, sherry, cinnamon, nutmeg, and ginger, and stir to combine. Pour the filling into the pastry shell, smooth the surface, and bake for 40 minutes, until set. If the edges of the pastry begin to brown too much during cooking, cover them with foil. Allow the pie to cool to room temperature and then decorate the top with the leaves.

filling

1 pound 2 ounces winter squash, chopped into small chunks

2 eggs, lightly beaten

¾ cup soft brown sugar

⅓ cup whipping cream

1 tablespoon sweet sherry

1 teaspoon ground cinnamon

½ teaspoon freshly grated nutmeg

½ teaspoon ground ginger

pastry

1¼ cups all-purpose flour

heaping ⅓ cup unsalted butter, cubed

2 teaspoons superfine sugar

⅓ cup iced water

1 egg yolk, lightly beaten, to glaze

1 tablespoon milk, to glaze

makes
12

Portuguese custard tarts

1¼ cups all-purpose flour

2 tablespoons white vegetable shortening, chopped and softened

2 tablespoons unsalted butter, chopped and softened

1 cup sugar

2 cups milk

¼ cup cornstarch

1 tablespoon instant vanilla pudding mix

4 egg yolks

1 teaspoon natural vanilla extract

Sift the flour into a bowl and add about ¾ cup water, or enough to form a soft dough. Gather the dough into a ball, then roll out on baking paper to form a 12 x 9½-inch rectangle. Spread the vegetable shortening over the surface. Roll up from the short edge to form a log. Roll the dough out into a rectangle again and spread with the butter. Roll up again into a log and slice into 12 even pieces. Working from the center outwards, use your fingertips to press each round out to a circle large enough to cover the base and side of twelve ⅓-cup muffin holes. Press into the holes and refrigerate while preparing the filling.

Put the sugar and ⅓ cup water in a saucepan and stir over low heat until the sugar dissolves. Stir together a little of the milk with the cornstarch and pudding mix to form a smooth paste. Add to the pan with the remaining milk, egg yolks, and vanilla. Stir over low heat until the mixture thickens. Transfer to a bowl, cover, and allow to cool.

Preheat the oven to 425°F. Divide the filling evenly among the pastry bases and bake for 25–30 minutes, or until the custard is set and the tops have browned. Cool in the pans for 10 minutes, then transfer to a wire rack.

78

serves
6–8

choux pastry

scant ¼ cup unsalted butter

¾ cup all-purpose flour, sifted

3 eggs, lightly beaten

filling

3 egg yolks

¼ cup superfine sugar

2 tablespoons all-purpose flour

1 cup milk

1 teaspoon natural vanilla extract

1 cup whipping cream, whipped

1½ cups raspberries or sliced strawberries, or a mixture of both

Paris–Brest

This wheel-shaped pastry was created in 1891 to commemorate a bicycle race between the French cities of Paris and Brest.

Preheat the oven to 415°F. Brush a large tray with melted butter or oil and line the tray with baking paper. Mark a 9-inch circle on the paper.

To make the pastry, stir the butter with ¾ cup water in a saucepan over low heat until the butter has melted and the mixture boils. Remove from the heat, add the flour all at once, and, using a wooden spoon, beat until smooth. Return to the heat and beat until the mixture thickens and comes away from the side of the pan. Remove from the heat and cool slightly. Transfer to a large bowl. Using electric beaters, add the egg gradually, beating until stiff and glossy. Place heaping tablespoons of mixture on the tray, touching each other, using the marked circle as a guide. Bake for 25–30 minutes, until browned and hollow sounding when the base is tapped. Turn off the oven and leave the pastry to dry inside.

To make the filling, whisk the egg yolks, sugar, and flour in a bowl until pale. Heat the milk in a saucepan until almost boiling. Gradually add to the egg mixture, stirring constantly. Return to the pan and stir constantly over medium heat until the mixture boils and thickens. Cook for another 2 minutes, stirring constantly. Remove from the heat and stir in the vanilla. Transfer to a bowl, cover

NOTE The pastry ring and the custard may both be made up to 4 hours in advance. Store the pastry ring in an airtight container, and refrigerate the custard until required. Assemble close to serving time.

the surface with plastic wrap to prevent a skin from forming, and set aside to cool.

To make the topping, combine all the ingredients in a heatproof bowl. Stand the bowl over a saucepan of simmering water and stir until the chocolate has melted and the mixture is smooth. Cool slightly.

To assemble, cut the pastry ring in half horizontally using a serrated knife. Remove any excess dough that remains in the center. Fold the whipped cream through the custard and spoon into the base of the pastry. Top with the fruit. Replace the remaining pastry half on top. Using a flat-bladed knife, spread the topping over the top of the pastry. Leave to set.

topping

scant 1 cup dark chocolate, chopped

2 tablespoons unsalted butter

1 tablespoon whipping cream

serves
8

Pineapple upside-down cake

1/3 cup unsalted butter, melted

½ cup soft brown sugar

15½ ounce can pineapple rings in natural juice

6 red glacé cherries

½ cup unsalted butter, extra, softened

¾ cup superfine sugar

2 eggs, lightly beaten

1 teaspoon natural vanilla extract

1½ cups self-rising flour

½ cup all-purpose flour

⅓ cup grated dried coconut

Preheat the oven to 350°F. Pour the melted butter into an 8-inch round pan, brushing some of it up the side, but leaving most on the base. Sprinkle the brown sugar over the base. Drain the pineapple, reserving ½ cup of the juice. Arrange the pineapple rings over the base of the pan (five on the outside and one in the center) and put a cherry in the center of each ring.

Cream the extra butter and caster sugar in a small bowl using electric beaters until light and fluffy. Add the egg gradually, beating thoroughly after each addition. Add the vanilla and beat until combined. Transfer to a large bowl. Using a metal spoon, fold in the sifted flours, then add the coconut and reserved pineapple juice. Stir until the mixture is just combined and almost smooth. Spoon the mixture into the pan over the pineapple rings and smooth the surface. Indent the center slightly with the back of a spoon to ensure the cake has a reasonably flat base. Bake for 50–60 minutes, or until a skewer inserted into the center of the cake comes out clean. Leave in the pan for 10 minutes before turning out onto a wire rack to cool.

Raspberry shortcake

shortcake pastry

1 cup all-purpose flour

⅓ cup confectioners' sugar

⅓ cup unsalted butter, chilled and chopped

1 egg yolk

½ teaspoon natural vanilla extract

½–1 tablespoon iced water

topping

6 cups fresh raspberries

¼ cup confectioners' sugar

⅓ cup redcurrant jelly

heavy cream, to serve

To make the pastry, sift the flour and confectioners' sugar into a large bowl. Using your fingertips, rub in the butter until the mixture resembles fine breadcrumbs. Add the egg yolk, vanilla, and enough of the iced water to make the ingredients come together, then mix to a dough with a flat-bladed knife, using a cutting action. Turn out onto a lightly floured work surface and gather together into a ball. Flatten slightly, wrap in plastic wrap, and refrigerate for 30 minutes.

Preheat the oven to 350°F. Roll out the pastry to fit a 4 x 13½-inch loose-based fluted tart pan and trim the edge. Prick all over with a fork and refrigerate for 20 minutes. Cover the pastry with baking paper and a layer of baking beads or uncooked rice. Bake for 15–20 minutes, or until golden. Remove the paper and beads and bake for another 15 minutes. Cool on a wire rack.

To make the topping, set aside 4 cups of the best berries and mash the rest with the confectioners' sugar. Just before serving, spread the mashed raspberries over the shortcake. Cover with the whole raspberries. Heat the redcurrant jelly in a small saucepan until melted and smooth. Use a soft pastry brush to coat the raspberries heavily with warm jelly. Cut into slices and serve with cream.

NOTE Shortcake is a classic American dish. It is usually made as a round of shortcake which is split, then filled or topped with fresh strawberries.

Ricotta and berry tartlets

pastry

1¼ cups all-purpose flour

⅓ cup ground almonds

1 tablespoon superfine sugar

⅓ cup unsalted butter, chilled and cubed

pinch of salt

1 egg yolk, at room temperature

filling

2½ cups mixed berries, such as raspberries, strawberries, and blueberries

1 egg, at room temperature

¼ cup superfine sugar

1 tablespoon lemon juice

scant ⅔ cup ricotta cheese

confectioners' sugar, for dusting

To make the pastry, put the flour, ground almonds, sugar, butter, and salt in a food processor. Process until the mixture resembles fine breadcrumbs. Add the egg yolk and 1 tablespoon of iced water. Process until the mixture just forms a ball, adding a little extra water if the pastry is too dry. Turn the pastry out onto a work surface. Flatten it into a disc, cover with plastic wrap, and refrigerate for 30 minutes.

Lightly grease six 3½-inch diameter, ¾-inch deep tartlet pans. Roll out the pastry on a lightly floured surface to a thickness of ⅛ inch. Cut out six 5-inch circles and place in the pans. Prick the base of the pastry with a fork and refrigerate for 10 minutes. Preheat the oven to 400°F.

To make the filling, hull any strawberries and chop any larger berries. Put the egg, superfine sugar, and lemon juice in a heatproof bowl and place over a saucepan of simmering water, making sure the base of the bowl doesn't touch the water. Whisk with an electric whisk for 5–6 minutes, or until light and creamy. Stir in the ricotta. Divide the berries among the tartlet cases and spoon over the ricotta mixture. Bake for 20–22 minutes, or until the pastry edges are golden brown. Serve warm or at room temperature, dusted with confectioners' sugar.

serves
6

Strawberry millefeuille

1 pound 2 ounce block puff
pastry, thawed

½ cup sugar

1 quantity pastry cream
(see page 181)

½ cup whipping cream

2 cups strawberries, cut into
quarters

confectioners' sugar, to dust

This dessert hides a whole lot of calories behind its
innocent pink and white façade. It's all the invisible
fat in the pastry and the pastry cream, of course.

Preheat the oven to 350°F. Roll out the puff pastry on a
sheet of baking paper into a rectangle about ¹⁄₁₆ inch thick.
Refrigerate for 15 minutes.

Put the sugar and ¾ cup water in a saucepan, boil for
5 minutes, then remove from the heat. Cut three 5 x
12-inch rectangles from the pastry and place on a large
cookie sheet. Prick with a fork, cover with baking paper,
and place a second cookie sheet on top to prevent the
pastry from rising. Bake for 6 minutes, then remove the
top cookie sheet and the baking paper. Brush the pastry
with the syrup and bake for 6 minutes more, or until
golden on top. Cool on a wire rack.

Whisk the pastry cream. Whip the cream and fold into
the pastry cream. Spread half of this mixture over one
pastry rectangle and top with half of the strawberries.
Place a second layer of pastry on top and spread with the
remaining cream and strawberries. Cover with the last
layer of pastry and dust with confectioners' sugar to serve.

Treacle tart

serves
6–8

shortcrust pastry

1¼ cups all-purpose flour

⅓ cup unsalted butter, chilled and chopped

2–3 tablespoons iced water

1 egg, lightly beaten, to glaze

filling

1 cup golden syrup or dark corn syrup

2 tablespoons unsalted butter

½ teaspoon ground ginger

1¾ cups fresh white breadcrumbs

confectioners' sugar, to dust

ice cream or cream, to serve

To make the pastry, sift the flour into a large bowl. Using your fingertips, rub in the butter until the mixture resembles fine breadcrumbs. Add almost all the iced water and mix to a firm dough, with a flat-bladed knife, using a cutting action. Add more water if the dough is too dry. Turn onto a lightly floured work surface and gather together into a ball. Cover with plastic wrap and refrigerate for 20 minutes.

Brush an 8-inch diameter tart pan with melted butter or oil. Roll out the pastry until large enough to fit the base and side of the pan, allowing an overhang of 1½ inches. Ease the pastry into the pan and trim by running a rolling pin firmly across the top of the pan. Reroll the trimmed pastry into a rectangle 4 x 8 inches. Using a sharp knife or fluted pastry wheel, cut into long strips ½ inch wide. Cover with plastic wrap and refrigerate for 20 minutes. Preheat the oven to 350°F.

To make the filling, combine the golden syrup, butter, and ginger in a small saucepan and stir over low heat until the butter melts. Stir in the breadcrumbs until combined. Pour the mixture into the pastry case. Lay half the pastry strips over the tart, starting at the center and working outwards. Lay the remaining strips over the tart to form a lattice pattern. Brush the lattice with beaten egg. Bake for 30 minutes, or until the pastry is lightly golden. Serve warm or at room temperature. Dust the top with confectioners' sugar and serve with ice cream or cream.

84

Danish pastries

2 teaspoons dried yeast

½ cup warm milk

I teaspoon superfine sugar

2 cups all-purpose flour

¼ cup superfine sugar, extra

I egg, lightly beaten

I teaspoon natural vanilla
  extract

I cup unsalted butter, chilled

NOTE Yeast needs
warmth and liquid to
activate it. The liquid
should be warm but not
hot. Store dried yeast in
a cool, dry place or in
the refrigerator. It will
keep for up to a year.

Stir the yeast, milk, and sugar together in a small bowl until dissolved. Leave in a warm, draft-free place for 10 minutes, or until bubbles appear on the surface. The mixture should be frothy and slightly increased in volume. If your yeast doesn't foam, it is dead, so you will have to discard it and start again. Sift the flour and ½ teaspoon salt into a large bowl and stir in the extra sugar. Make a well in the center and add the yeast, egg, and vanilla. Mix to a firm dough. Turn out onto a lightly floured surface and knead for 10 minutes to form a smooth, elastic dough. Place the dough in a lightly greased bowl, cover, and set aside in a warm place for I hour, or until doubled in size. Meanwhile, roll the cold butter between two sheets of baking paper to a 6 x 8-inch rectangle and then refrigerate until required.

Gently punch down the dough and knead for I minute. Roll out to a 10 x 12-inch rectangle. Put the butter in the center of the dough and fold up the bottom and top of the dough over the butter to join in the center. Seal the edges with a rolling pin. Give the dough a quarter-turn clockwise, then roll out to a 8 x 17¾-inch rectangle. Fold over the top third of the pastry, then the bottom third, and give another quarter-turn clockwise. Cover and refrigerate for 30 minutes. Repeat the rolling, folding, turning, and chilling four more times. Wrap in plastic wrap and chill for at least 2 hours.

To make the pastry cream, put the sugar, egg yolks, and flours in a saucepan and whisk to combine. Pour the hot milk over the flour and whisk until smooth. Bring to the boil over moderate heat, stirring all the time, until the mixture boils and thickens. Cover and set aside.

NOTE Instead of apricots, you could use drained tinned morello cherries and cherry jam.

pastry cream

2 tablespoons superfine sugar

2 egg yolks

2 teaspoons all-purpose flour

2 teaspoons cornstarch

½ cup hot milk

15 ounce can apricot halves, drained

1 egg, lightly beaten

⅓ cup flaked almonds

¼ cup apricot jam, to glaze

Preheat the oven to 400°F and line two cookie sheets with baking paper. On a lightly floured surface, roll the dough into a rectangle or square ⅛ inch thick. Cut the dough into 4-inch squares and place on the cookie sheets. Spoon I tablespoon of pastry cream into the center of each square and top with two apricot halves. Brush one corner with the beaten egg and draw up that corner and the diagonally opposite one to touch in the middle between the apricots. Press firmly in the center. Leave in a warm place to prove for 30 minutes. Brush each pastry with egg and sprinkle with almonds. Bake for 15–20 minutes, or until golden. Cool on wire racks. Melt the apricot jam with I tablespoon water in a saucepan and then strain. Brush the tops of the apricots with the hot glaze and serve.

Vanilla slice

1 pound 2 ounce block puff pastry, thawed

1 cup superfine sugar

¾ cup cornstarch

½ cup instant vanilla pudding mix

4 cups whipping cream

¼ cup unsalted butter, cubed

2 teaspoons natural vanilla extract

3 egg yolks

icing

1½ cups confectioners' sugar

¼ cup passionfruit pulp

1 tablespoon unsalted butter, melted

Preheat the oven to 415°F. Grease two cookie sheets with oil. Line the base and sides of a shallow 9-inch square cake pan with foil, leaving the foil hanging over on two opposite sides. Divide the pastry in half, roll each piece to a 10-inch square about ⅛ inch thick, and place each one on a prepared tray. Prick all over with a fork and bake for 8 minutes, or until golden. Trim each pastry sheet to a 9-inch square. Place one sheet, top side down, in the prepared cake pan.

Combine the sugar, cornstarch, and pudding mix in a saucepan. Gradually add the cream and stir until smooth. Place over medium heat and stir constantly for 2 minutes, or until the mixture boils and thickens. Add the butter and vanilla and stir until smooth. Remove from the heat and whisk in the egg yolks until combined. Spread the custard over the pastry in the pan and cover with the remaining pastry, top side down. Allow to cool.

To make the frosting, combine the confectioners' sugar, passionfruit pulp, and melted butter in a small bowl and stir together until smooth.

Lift the slice out, using the foil as handles, spread the frosting over the top and leave it to set before carefully cutting into nine squares with a serrated knife.

makes
18 pieces

2⅓ cups superfine sugar

1½ teaspoons finely grated lemon zest

¼ cup honey

¼ cup lemon juice

2 tablespoons orange blossom water

heaping 1½ cups walnuts, finely chopped

heaping 1½ cups pistachio nuts, finely chopped

1⅓ cups almonds, finely chopped

2 tablespoons superfine sugar, extra

2 teaspoons ground cinnamon

heaping ¾ cup unsalted butter, melted

13 ounces filo pastry

Baklava

Put the sugar, lemon zest, and 1½ cups water in a saucepan and stir over high heat until the sugar has dissolved, then boil for 5 minutes. Reduce the heat to low and simmer for 5 minutes, or until the syrup has thickened slightly and just coats the back of a spoon. Add the honey, lemon juice, and orange blossom water, and cook for 2 minutes. Remove from the heat and leave to cool completely.

Preheat the oven to 325°F. Combine the nuts, extra sugar, and cinnamon in a bowl. Brush the base and sides of a 10¾ x 12-inch ovenproof dish or cake pan with the melted butter. Cover the base with a single layer of filo pastry and brush lightly with the butter, folding in any overhanging edges. Continue layering the filo, brushing each new layer with butter and folding in the edges until ten sheets have been used. Keep the unused filo under a damp dish towel.

Sprinkle half the nut mixture over the pastry and pat down evenly. Repeat the layering and buttering of five more filo sheets, sprinkle with the remaining nuts, then continue to layer and butter the remaining sheets, including the top layer. Press down with your hands so the pastry and nuts stick to each other. Using a large, sharp knife, cut into diamond shapes, ensuring you cut through to the bottom layer. Pour any remaining butter evenly over the top and smooth with your hands. Bake for 30 minutes, then reduce the oven to 300°F, and cook for another 30 minutes.

Immediately cut through the original diamond markings, then strain the syrup evenly over the top. Cool completely before lifting the diamonds out onto a serving platter.

TIP To achieve the right texture, it is important for the baklava to be piping hot and the syrup cool when pouring the syrup.

COOKIES, SWEET TREATS, & Candies

Florentines

makes 12

¼ cup unsalted butter

¼ cup soft brown sugar

2 teaspoons honey

¼ cup roughly chopped flaked almonds

2 tablespoons chopped dried apricots

2 tablespoons chopped glacé cherries

2 tablespoons mixed candied citrus peel

⅓ cup all-purpose flour, sifted

¾ cup chopped dark chocolate

Preheat the oven to 350°F. Melt the butter, sugar, and honey in a saucepan until the butter has melted and all the ingredients are combined. Remove from the heat and add the almonds, apricots, glacé cherries, mixed citrus peel, and the flour. Mix well.

Grease two cookie sheets and line with baking paper. Place level tablespoons of the mixture on the trays, allowing room for spreading. Reshape and flatten the biscuits into 2-inch rounds before cooking.

Bake for 10 minutes, or until lightly browned. Cool on the trays, then allow to cool completely on a wire rack.

Put the chocolate in a heatproof bowl. Half-fill a saucepan with water, bring to the boil, then remove from the heat and set the bowl over the pan (don't let the bowl touch the water or the chocolate will get too hot and stiffen). Stir occasionally until melted.

Spread the chocolate on the bottom of each florentine and, using a fork, make a wavy pattern in the chocolate before it sets. Leave to set before serving.

88

makes
12

Ginger shortbread

1 cup unsalted butter, softened

½ cup confectioners' sugar

2 cups all-purpose flour

1 teaspoon ground ginger

⅓ cup chopped crystallized ginger

If you really need an excuse to eat more butter, sugar, and flour, then shortbread is the simplest and yet one of the most delicious ways to indulge.

Preheat the oven to 300°F. Line a 9-inch round or square baking pan, or a cookie sheet, with baking paper.

Cream the butter and sugar in a small bowl using electric beaters until light and fluffy. Sift the flour into the bowl with the ground ginger. Add the chopped ginger and mix with a flat-bladed knife, using a cutting action, to form a soft dough. Gently gather together and press into the pan, or shape into a round about ½ inch thick on the cookie sheet. Prick the surface all over with a fork and score into 12 wedges.

Bake for 40–45 minutes, or until lightly golden. While still warm, cut into 12 wedges. Cool in the pan, or on the tray for about 3 minutes before transferring to a wire rack to cool completely. Store in an airtight container.

makes
about 60

½ cup unsalted butter, cubed and softened

2 cups soft brown sugar

1 teaspoon natural vanilla extract

2 eggs

heaping ⅓ cup dark chocolate, melted

⅓ cup milk

2¾ cups all-purpose flour

2 tablespoons unsweetened cocoa powder

2 teaspoons baking powder

¼ teaspoon ground allspice (pimento)

pinch of salt

⅔ cup chopped pecan nuts

confectioners' sugar, to coat

Crackle cookies

Lightly grease two cookie sheets. Beat the butter, sugar, and vanilla until light and creamy. Beat in the eggs, one at a time. Stir in the chocolate and milk.

Sift the flour, cocoa, baking powder, allspice, and salt into the butter mixture and mix well. Stir the pecans through. Refrigerate for at least 3 hours, or overnight.

Preheat the oven to 350°F. Roll tablespoons of the mixture into balls and then roll each in confectioners' sugar to coat.

Place well apart on the trays. Bake for 20–25 minutes, or until lightly browned. Cool slightly on the trays, then transfer to a wire rack to cool completely.

NOTE These biscuits will keep, stored in an airtight container, for up to 3 days.

makes
about 40

Chocolate chip cookies

1½ cups all-purpose flour

¾ cup unsweetened cocoa powder

1½ cups soft brown sugar

¾ cup unsalted butter, cubed

1 cup chopped dark chocolate

3 eggs, at room temperature, lightly beaten

1½ cups milk or dark chocolate chips

Preheat the oven to 350°F. Line two cookie sheets with baking paper.

Sift the flour and cocoa into a large bowl, add the sugar, and make a well in the center.

Put the butter and chocolate in a small heatproof bowl. Bring a saucepan of water to the boil, then remove the pan from the heat. Set the bowl over the saucepan. Stir occasionally until the chocolate and butter have melted and the mixture is smooth.

Add the butter and chocolate mixture and the egg to the dry ingredients. Mix well with a wooden spoon, but do not overmix. Stir in the chocolate chips. Drop tablespoons of the mixture onto the trays, allowing room for spreading. Bake for 7–10 minutes, or until firm to touch. Cool on the trays for 5 minutes before transferring to a wire rack to cool completely.

makes
20

Chocolate peppermint creams

¼ cup unsalted butter

¼ cup superfine sugar

½ cup all-purpose flour

⅓ cup self-rising flour

2 tablespoons unsweetened cocoa powder

2 tablespoons milk

peppermint cream

1 egg white

1¾ cups confectioners' sugar, sifted

2–3 drops natural peppermint extract or oil, to taste

chocolate topping

1 cup chopped dark chocolate

1 cup dark chocolate buttons

Preheat the oven to 350°F. Line two cookie sheets with baking paper.

Cream the butter and sugar in a small bowl using electric beaters until light and fluffy. Add the sifted flours and cocoa alternately with the milk. Mix with a flat-bladed knife, using a cutting action, until the mixture forms a soft dough. Turn out onto a floured surface and gather together into a rough ball. Cut the dough in half. Roll each half between two sheets of baking paper to 1/16 inch thick. Slide onto a tray and refrigerate for 15 minutes, or until firm. Cut the dough into rounds using a 1½-inch round cutter, rerolling the dough scraps and cutting more rounds. Place on the trays, allowing room for spreading. Bake for 10 minutes, or until firm. Transfer to a wire rack to cool completely.

To make the peppermint cream, put the egg white in a small, clean, dry bowl. Whisk in the confectioners' sugar, 2 tablespoons at a time, using electric beaters on low speed. Add more confectioners' sugar, if necessary, until a soft dough forms. Turn the dough out onto a surface dusted with confectioners' sugar and knead in enough confectioners' sugar so that the dough is not sticky. Knead in the peppermint extract.

Roll a teaspoon of peppermint cream into a ball, and flatten slightly. Sandwich between two biscuits, pressing

NOTE For chocolate orange creams, replace the peppermint oil with orange oil.

together lightly. Repeat with the remaining filling and biscuits, keeping the filling covered as you work.

To make the topping, put the chopped chocolate and the chocolate buttons in a heatproof bowl. Half-fill a saucepan with water and bring to the boil. Remove from the heat and place the bowl over the pan, making sure the base of the bowl does not touch the water. Stir occasionally until the chocolate is melted. Remove from the heat and allow to cool slightly. Use a fork to dip the biscuits into the chocolate and allow any excess to drain away. Place on a tray lined with baking paper to set.

Chocolate orange fudge

14 ounce can sweetened condensed milk

3 tablespoons unsalted butter, cubed

1⅓ cups finely chopped orange-flavored dark chocolate

1⅓ cups finely chopped dark chocolate (54 per cent cocoa solids)

Line the base and sides of a 7-inch square cake pan with baking paper, extending the paper over two opposite sides for easy removal later.

Place the condensed milk and butter in a heavy-based saucepan and cook over low heat, stirring occasionally, until the butter has melted. Bring just to a simmer, stirring frequently. Remove from the heat and set aside for 5 minutes to cool slightly. Add all the chocolate and stir until the chocolate has melted.

Working quickly, pour the fudge mixture into the prepared pan and use the back of a metal spoon to smooth the surface. Refrigerate for 4 hours, or until firm.

Use the paper to remove the fudge from the pan and cut it into 1¼ inch squares.

NOTE Fudge squares will keep, separated by baking paper, in an airtight container in the refrigerator, for up to 1 month.

makes
30 pieces

Creamy coconut ice

2 cups confectioners' sugar

¼ teaspoon cream of tartar

14 ounce can sweetened
  condensed milk

3½ cups grated dried coconut

2–3 drops red food coloring

Grease an 8-inch square cake pan and line the base and sides with baking paper, extending the paper over two opposite sides for easy removal later.

Sift the confectioners' sugar and cream of tartar into a bowl. Make a well in the center and add the condensed milk. Using a wooden spoon, stir in half the coconut, then the remaining coconut. Mix well, using your hands. Divide the mixture in half and add a few drops of red food coloring to tint one half pink. Using your hands, knead the color through evenly.

Press the pink mixture evenly over the base of the pan, then cover with the white mixture and press down firmly. Refrigerate for 1–2 hours, or until firm. Remove from the pan, remove the paper and cut into 30 pieces. Store in an airtight container in a cool place for up to 3 weeks.

NOTE This children's party favorite is traditionally colored pink, but you can use another color if you prefer. Or make two batches, each of a different color.

94

makes
about 25

Rum truffles

These grown-up confections are pretty much solid chocolate, cream, and butter. They're tiny, and so tempting that it's easy to eat them in large quantities.

1⅓ cups finely chopped dark chocolate

¼ cup cream

2 tablespoons unsalted butter

½ cup (50 g) chocolate cake crumbs

2 teaspoons dark rum

½ cup chocolate sprinkles

Line a cookie sheet with foil. Place the chocolate in a heatproof bowl. Combine the cream and butter in a saucepan and stir over low heat until the butter melts and the mixture is just boiling. Pour the hot mixture over the chocolate and stir until the chocolate melts and the mixture is smooth.

Stir in cake crumbs and rum. Refrigerate for 20 minutes, stirring occasionally, or until firm enough to handle. Roll heaped teaspoons of the mixture into balls.

Spread the chocolate sprinkles on a sheet of baking paper. Roll each truffle in the sprinkles, then place on the tray. Refrigerate for 30 minutes, or until firm. Serve in small paper cases, if desired.

These truffles are great to serve with coffee after a meal. They can be rolled in unsweetened cocoa powder instead of chocolate spinkles, if you prefer.

Nougat

makes
2 pounds
4 ounces

2 cups sugar

1 cup light corn syrup

½ cup honey

¼ teaspoon salt

2 egg whites

1 teaspoon natural vanilla
extract

½ cup unsalted butter,
softened

⅓ cup almonds, unblanched
and toasted

½ cup candied cherries

Grease a 7 x 11-inch baking dish and line it with baking paper. Put the sugar, corn syrup, honey, ¼ cup water, and the salt in a heavy-based saucepan and stir over low heat until dissolved. Bring to the boil and cook at a rolling boil for 8 minutes, or until the mixture reaches 225°F on a candy thermometer. The correct temperature is very important, otherwise the mixture will not set properly.

Whisk the egg whites in a bowl with electric beaters until stiff peaks form. Slowly pour one-quarter of the sugar syrup onto the egg whites in a thin stream and whisk for up to 5 minutes, or until the mixture holds its shape. Put the remaining syrup over the heat and cook for 2 minutes (watch that it doesn't burn), or until a small amount forms brittle threads when dropped in cold water, or until the mixture reaches 315°F on a candy thermometer. Pour slowly onto the meringue mixture with the beaters running and whisk until the mixture is very thick.

Add the vanilla and butter and beat for 5 minutes more. Stir in the almonds and cherries with a metal spoon. Spoon the mixture into the pan and smooth the top with a palette knife. Refrigerate for at least 4 hours, or until firm. Turn out onto a large chopping board and cut into ¾ x 1½-inch pieces. Wrap each piece in cellophane and store in the refrigerator.

96

Rocky road

2¾ cups pink and white
marshmallows, halved

1 cup roughly chopped
unsalted peanuts

½ cup candied cherries,
halved

1 cup shredded coconut

2⅓ cups chopped dark
chocolate

What you see is what you get—a solid and entirely
satisfying slab of nuts, chocolate, marshmallows,
and cherries.

Line the base and two opposite sides of an 8 inch square
cake pan with foil.

Combine the marshmallows, peanuts, cherries, and
coconut. Put the chocolate in a heatproof bowl and set it
over a saucepan of simmering water. Don't let the bowl
touch the water, or the chocolate will get too hot and
stiffen. Stir occasionally until just melted and smooth.
Add the chocolate to the marshmallow mixture and toss
together until combined.

Spoon into the pan and press evenly over the base to
remove any air bubbles. Refrigerate for several hours, or
until set. Carefully lift the rocky road out of the pan, then
peel away the foil and cut it into 30 pieces.

Peanut brittle

With butter, handfuls of nuts, and three types of sugar, this brittle isn't just luscious—it's also the sort of candy that puts dentists' children through private school.

Line the base and sides of a shallow 10 x 12-inch jelly roll pan with foil or baking paper. Grease the foil with melted butter or oil.

Combine the sugars, corn syrup, and ½ cup water in a large, heavy-based pan. Stir over medium heat without boiling until the sugar has completely dissolved. Brush the sugar crystals from the side of the pan with a wet pastry brush. Add the butter and stir until melted. Bring to the boil and cook without stirring for 15–20 minutes. The mixture must reach 250°F on a sugar thermometer, or until a little mixture dropped in water is brittle and not sticky. Remove from the heat.

Add the peanuts and fold in lightly, tilting the pan to help mix; don't overmix or the toffee will crystallize. Pour into the pan and smooth the surface with a buttered spatula. Leave the pan on a wire rack for the brittle to cool. Break into pieces when almost set. Store in an airtight container for up to 3 weeks.

makes
about
1 pound

97

2 cups sugar

1 cup soft brown sugar

½ cup dark corn syrup

¼ cup butter

2½ cups roasted, unsalted peanuts (or any other type or combination of roasted, unsalted nuts)

serves
12

Honey, nut, and chocolate wafers

heaping ⅓ cup butter, cubed

¾ cup superfine sugar

¼ cup runny honey

½ cup all-purpose flour

2 egg whites

½ cup unsalted macadamia nuts, halved

½ cup roasted skinned hazelnuts, halved

½ cup roughly chopped dark chocolate

Whether eaten on their own or used to garnish another dessert, these nut-studded dainties are enticing. Go on, they're wafer thin.

Preheat the oven to 350°F. Lightly oil three large cookie sheets. (If you only have one sheet, you will need to bake one batch at a time.) Cover each cookie sheet with a sheet of baking paper.

In a food processor, process the butter, sugar, honey, flour, and egg whites until the mixture is well blended and smooth.

Using a metal spatula, spread one-third of the mixture evenly and thinly over the entire surface of each cookie sheet. Or, if the mixture is too difficult to spread, tilt the pan so that the mixture flows evenly over the base. Scatter each batch with one-third of the combined macadamia nuts, hazelnuts, and chocolate. Bake for 10–12 minutes, or until evenly colored to a deep golden brown. Cool on the tray until crisp, then break into large pieces.

These wafers are good to serve with coffee, or on top of a creamy dessert. They will last for a couple of weeks in an airtight container.

99

Caramel popcorn balls

2 tablespoons oil

½ cup popping corn

¾ cup superfine sugar

⅓ cup unsalted butter

2 tablespoons honey

2 tablespoons whipping cream

Heat the oil in a large saucepan over medium heat. Add the corn and cover with a lid. Cook for 5 minutes, or until the popping stops, shaking the pan occasionally. Tip the popcorn into a big bowl.

Put the sugar, butter, honey, and cream in a small saucepan. Stir over medium heat, without boiling, until the sugar has completely dissolved. Bring to the boil and boil, without stirring, for 5 minutes.

Pour the caramel over the popcorn and mix together. Leave to cool a little, then rub some oil over your hands and mold the popcorn into 50 small balls. Put on a wire rack to set.

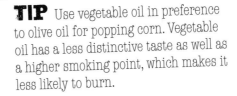

TIP Use vegetable oil in preference to olive oil for popping corn. Vegetable oil has a less distinctive taste as well as a higher smoking point, which makes it less likely to burn.

makes
about 60

Maple and pecan cookies

¾ cup unsalted butter, softened

I cup soft brown sugar

¼ cup maple syrup

I teaspoon natural vanilla extract

I egg

2¼ cups all-purpose flour

I teaspoon baking powder

I cup finely chopped pecans

whole pecans, to decorate

It's not the individual ingredients themselves that are the trouble here, it's how good they are together. It's just too hard to stop at one!

Cream the butter and sugar in a small bowl using electric beaters until light and fluffy. Add the maple syrup, vanilla, and egg, and beat until well combined. Transfer to a large bowl and add the sifted flour and baking powder. Using a flat-bladed knife, mix to a soft dough. Gather together, then divide the mixture into two portions.

Place one portion of the dough on a sheet of baking paper and press lightly until the dough is 12 inches long and 1½ inches thick. Roll neatly into a log shape, then roll the log in the chopped pecans. Repeat the process with the other portion of dough and refrigerate for 30 minutes, or until firm.

Preheat the oven to 350°F. Line two cookie sheets with baking paper. Cut the logs into slices about ½ inch thick. Press a whole pecan into the top of each cookie. Place on the prepared trays, leaving about 1¼ inches between the biscuits. Bake for 10–15 minutes, or until golden. Cool on the trays for 3 minutes before transferring to a wire rack to cool completely. When cool, store in an airtight container.

makes
about 25

Monte creams

½ cup unsalted butter, softened

½ cup superfine sugar

¼ cup milk

1½ cups self-rising flour

¼ cup instant vanilla pudding mix, plus extra

⅓ cup grated dried coconut

filling

scant ⅓ cup unsalted butter, softened

⅔ cup confectioners' sugar

2 teaspoons milk

⅓ cup strawberry or raspberry jam

Preheat the oven to 350°F. Line two cookie sheets with baking paper. Cream the butter and sugar in a small bowl using electric beaters until light and fluffy. Add the milk and beat until combined. Sift the flour and pudding mix and add to the bowl with the coconut. Mix to form a soft dough.

Roll 2 teaspoons of the mixture into balls. Place on the trays and press with a fork. Dip the fork in the extra pudding mix occasionally to prevent it from sticking. Bake for 15–20 minutes, or until just golden. Transfer to a wire rack to cool completely before filling.

To make the filling, beat the butter and confectioners' sugar in a small bowl using electric beaters until light and creamy. Beat in the milk. Spread one cookie with ½ teaspoon of the filling and one with ½ teaspoon of jam, then press them together. Repeat with the remaining cookies, filling, and jam.

INDEX

INDEX

101 DESSERTS TO EAT BEFORE YOU DIE(t)

Thunder Bay Press

An imprint of the Baker & Taylor Publishing Group

10350 Barnes Canyon Road, San Diego, CA 92121

www.thunderbaybooks.com

ISBN-13: 978-1-60710-214-4
ISBN-10: 1-60710-214-5

Printed in China.

1 2 3 4 5 15 14 13 12 11

IMPORTANT: Those who might be at risk from the effects of salmonella poisoning (elderly people, pregnant women, young children and those suffering from immune deficiency diseases) should consult their doctor with any concerns about eating raw eggs.